RAISED BY
THE WORLD

RAISED BY THE WORLD

My Path to Becoming Zambia's First PGA Golf Professional

Vincent Kabaso, PGA

Library of Congress Control Number:		2020919249
ISBN:	Hardcover	978-1-6641-3012-8
	Softcover	978-1-6641-3011-1
	eBook	978-1-6641-3010-4

Print information available on the last page.

Rev. date: 10/14/2020

To order additional copies of this book, contact:
Xlibris
844-714-8691
www.Xlibris.com
Orders@Xlibris.com
817992

This book is dedicated to anyone living with a dream that seems impossible — to let them know anything is possible. It is also dedicated to the people who have given themselves in service or otherwise, to make this world a better place; people like Jonathan MacDonald. To my dad for introducing me to golf, and my mom, brothers and sisters for their support.

ACKNOWLEDGMENT

I received great insight from some amazing people while putting this book together. Annie Marshall deserves great credit for her wonderful editing skills. Levy Sakala in Zambia, Steve Hennessey at Golf digest, and Bob Denney from the PGA of America gave me their time, effort, and insight.

Lastly, my wife and kids whose love inspired me in many ways as I wrote this book. Above all, I am indebted to God who continues to give me peace of mind, and hope for the future especially in times of adversity.

FOREWORD

Dreamers are a dime a dozen. However, when you are willing to do whatever it takes to make that dream come true, you are on your way to making that dream become a reality. Vincent Kabaso is one of those who was willing to take the risk to realize his dream, and because of that, in my eyes, Vincent is truly *invincible*.

My name is Vince Papale and in 1976 I did something that people deemed impossible, but like Vincent, I proved that the impossible can be made possible. The Disney movie *Invincible* is all about that dream and it is simply a metaphor for anybody who shoots for the stars . . . just like Vincent Kabaso! Against all odds and obstacles, Vincent proved the doubters wrong, and got the last laugh, by becoming the first PGA golfer from Zambia.

To have the vision at the age of nine and with the help of his father—his mentor—they were able to game plan that image into reality that is the heart of this truly inspiring book. Vincent's journey is the substance of champions of any age to emulate in their pursuit of having their wildest dream come true.

The willingness of Vincent to pay the price to become a PGA Pro is an example for us all, proving that attitude, perseverance, trust, hard work, and resilience really can turn anyone's vision into victory.

Vincent is a shining star for those who fantasize to have that impossible dream come true!

- Vince Papale

1

Tee Box

The starting point to a round of golf

*N*obody used an alarm clock in my family. It was the loud clucking of my mom's chickens that woke us up in the morning. Or if we missed the crowing from our rooster, it was either the seven o'clock siren signaling a shift change from the copper mines or the odd explosion at the fourteenth shaft open pit mine that would wake us up. Once awake, the sounds of the town would begin, as neighbors and local traders started making their way down the congested, dusty streets.

At eight years old, I was typically roused by the rooster, especially because, after we moved from the upper sixth section of the miner's compound to a new housing development community called Kamirenda near the central business area of Luanshya township, my mom started letting the chickens sleep inside the house. Much to my dad's displeasure, we had close to twenty chickens living in our kitchen at one point. Sometimes, I woke up to find the mess they made in the kitchen before Mom cleaned it up.

Childhood home in Roan

In our Kamirenda house, we had three bedrooms for ten people to sleep in. My youngest sister, Anna-Chomba, slept with my parents while the rest of us were divided into the other two bedrooms. In the girls' room, my eldest sister, Beatrice, slept on a blanket on the floor while my remaining sisters, Regina, Josephine, and Flavia, slept together on two single metal beds we pushed together. My older brothers, Albert and Sydney, shared one bed and laid a couple of blankets on the floor for me in the boys' room.

Although we were a little cramped, this situation was preferable to previous arrangements. Our old house in Roan, a compound that housed lower-income mine workers, was only a two-bedroom house. There, my brothers and I used to sleep on the living room floor. Albert and Sydney would push the table to one side of the room and the couch to the other in order to create enough space to spread a mattress for us to share.

In addition to having less space, our first house only had an outdoor bathroom. While this was manageable for me during the daytime, it posed a problem at night. As a child, I was terrified of witches and their vessels—owls and cats. This remains a common superstition in Zambia and Africa. I inherited it from older friends and family members. If cats or owls were spotted near a particular house,

2

the community would gossip that whoever lived inside were witches. I have not mended my relationship with cats since. Not wanting to risk any chance of crossing paths with a witch on a trip to the bathroom at night, I would cut open a two-and-a-half-liter container and keep it nearby to pee in. If I didn't have access to a container, I would simply wet the bed. That is how superstitious and fearful I was. This issue persisted for many years to the point that my parents thought it was an ailment. We were all relieved when we moved into our bigger house with an indoor bathroom, complete with shower and toilet, and my nightly bed-wetting ended.

Running water felt like a miracle anytime it came. However, even when we upgraded to our larger house and had an indoor bathroom, our shower didn't have enough pressure to supply running water. Instead, we dug a well about fifty yards deep on our property. My mom was adamant that we all take baths in the morning before school, so my siblings and I would run outside to the well and line up to draw bathing water before breakfast.

If we were lucky and there was time, Mom would let us heat up the water. Otherwise, we were forced to take a cold bath each morning. The drama of racing the clock and each other often led to fights between me and my sisters. I was always the last one to wake up, meaning I was usually last in line to take a bath. But more often than not, rather than subjecting myself to a cold bath, I would wipe my face and feet with a towel and then apply Vaseline to get ready for school.

We also used well water for drinking. This water needed to be drawn early in the morning; otherwise, it became muddy as our neighbors drew water from our well throughout the day. My mom drew a dead rat from the well one time, but it didn't stop us from using the water for cooking or even drinking. We boiled the water or treated it with chlorine to kill the germs, and it still tasted better than what was coming out of our tap.

After washing, I would return to the house and grab some dry bread from the kitchen for breakfast. My family typically went through two loaves each morning. Half the time, Dad brought home

Shoprite bread, and the other half of the time, I or one of my siblings would run to a nearby community stand that sold sliced bread. These stands could be found at almost every street corner. On some unlucky days, Dad didn't have money for breakfast, so we'd have to go to school without food.

The previous year, my dad was retrenched from the mine, which meant that his role had become redundant. Understandably, with a family of ten, money was a little tight after that. Although his retrenchment was somewhat unexpected, it wasn't an uncommon occurrence in our community. The mine was constantly being restructured, and unreliable copper prices reminded everyone that steady employment was a privilege.

The one good thing that came out of my dad's sudden unemployment was the benefits package he received as compensation. The national economic system didn't provide structured retirement plans; instead, workers received a lump sum and were immediately cut off from company insurance. My parents decided to use that money to build us our new house near the central business area of Luanshya township, as opposed to returning to the village as many others did. Living in town was meant to grant us a more modern lifestyle than we would have in the village; our home could have electric lights instead of candles, a cooker instead of firewood for making meals, and access to television.

However, we toiled for a while as we made this transition. My dad's package wasn't enough to finish building our home when we moved in. Without a roof or ceiling board installed over half of the house, we weathered some storms that the asbestos roofing was not meant to handle. The rain was loud, and leaks were unavoidable. We did not have electricity for the first year, so during that time, my mom cooked meals on a brazier while we sat, listened to stories in the dark, and contended with mosquito bites.

Infront of childhood home at 4 years old

As a child, I believed that this was just the way it was, and I never really thought about what we could or couldn't afford beyond what I was exposed to in my daily life. My mental prospects were limited to my neighborhood, which exposed me to nothing more than other huge families who also struggled to make ends meet. I entertained the idea that other people lived better lives than we did, but I didn't dwell on it. As far as I was concerned, at least my family had our own house. And even if our house was only halfway finished, most of my neighbors were squatting in completely unfinished or deserted buildings. So around us, we were the ones better off.

After eating breakfast, Sydney, Josephine, Flavia, and I would join the other kids from our neighborhood outside to walk to school. Everyone who was between the ages of five and fourteen went to the same government school, Mpelembe Primary School. In those days, you had to be a minimum of five years old *and* be able to pull your arm over your head to touch your ear on the other side to enroll in school.

The walk took about thirty-five minutes. We were a daily caravan of about fifteen kids. One time when I walked home alone, I got lost and had to trade the cream doughnut my mom packed for my lunch in exchange for directions, so I preferred to travel as part of a group.

Our route first took us along a gravel road adjacent to a Darg Hammarskjold school for the handicapped. This was a Catholic school, which was well-fenced and housed a few thousand students from across Zambia. Then we cut over to the railroad tracks, which we followed through the back end of Luanshya all the way to school.

To me, Luanshya seemed to be a microcosm of Zambia; to our standard, we had a wealthy minority, and the majority of people lived in poverty. The affluent and powerful in this bustling copper mining town lived in opulent senior personnel homes, which were gated and named after historical or noteworthy events or people. The streets in these neighborhoods had pleasant, botanical names like Poinsettia, Jakaranda, Keria, Wisteria, and Eucalyptus. Lower-income mine workers, on the other hand, lived in compounds like Roan and Mpatamatu. These compounds provided company housing to general workers and their families. Even more crowded, the rest of the town was squeezed into non-mining compounds like Mikomfwa and Kalala. The local people residing there maintained traditional trades like carpentry, bricklaying, and craftsmanship. Some worked in markets, selling fresh vegetables; indigenous fruits; and dried, harvested fish. One part of town housed a now-extinct clothing manufacturing plant called Scerios, and the business of second-hand clothing was slowly becoming a new norm.

Family picture

It was a good thing that the neighborhood kids, my siblings, and I stayed on the train tracks, so we couldn't get distracted by people or opportunities in town. As it was, we typically arrived right before the siren went off, signaling the beginning of class. We always hustled if we thought we were cutting it close because a supervising teacher was assigned each week to wait outside the school gate and punish latecomers. Any boy who arrived after the start of class could expect five ruthless whips on his rear-end while girls would have their hands smacked with a chalkboard duster.

Every Monday and Friday before classes began, all of the students paraded outside, military-style, and said the Lord's Prayer. Then we mumbled our way through Zambia's national anthem. While I definitely knew the tune, the words remained a mystery to me for many years. Teachers and administrators would make any announcements, and then the same teacher who punished latecomers would now identify all the scruffy-looking kids and embarrass them in front of everyone for not meeting the school's standard. This was either done verbally (by making fun of messy hair or wrinkled uniforms) or physically (by cutting out huge chunks of hair with a pair of scissors to ensure they got a haircut by the following day). After this biweekly torture, it was a sprint to pick out the best seat in class.

The environment and lifestyle I was exposed to at this time taught me to follow instructions, to not ask questions, and to do as I was told. As a young boy, I never talked back to a teacher or disobeyed an order that was given to me in the classroom or at home. My way of life was to respect my elders and authority and to trust that they knew what was best.

However, going to school was always perceived as more of a temporary rite of passage rather than an opportunity to improve my life. Nobody ever told me that being in school had significance, so I did the bare minimum required. Being in class felt like being in prison.

Luckily, our school schedule was split between grades with some kids attending in the morning and others in the afternoon, which meant I did have a lot of free time. Most days, I would go to school, come back home, change into casual clothes, and either pick up a pair of catapults to go hunting or join other kids at the local improvised soccer field where we played barefoot with a plastic soccer ball.

My family had lunch at around one o'clock in the afternoon, and because of my other siblings' schedules, we all ate together. If anyone was late coming home for lunch, it was understood there wouldn't be any food left. I did my best to make sure I was home on time, and if my sisters knew I was playing soccer nearby, they were kind enough to shout my name at the far end of the field, so I would realize the hour and run home with them.

Lunch was usually *nshima*; other times, we had sweet potatoes, which, unlike bread, was very cost-effective. My dad would buy sweet potatoes in bulk in a 110-pound sack that would last us for weeks. Given how frequently we ate them, my sisters eventually learned how to cook sweet potatoes in all kinds of ways: mixed with

8

onions and tomatoes, sliced up and fried, garnished with roasted peanuts, or boiled with the skins on to name a few.

School didn't really have any extracurricular activities for younger students although we sometimes went back to participate in the mandatory school cleaning program, which required you to bring a tool from home to help maintain the property. You could bring a slasher, a plow, or grass-cutting scissors. If I didn't have school in the afternoon and wasn't forced to perform manual labor, I would go hunting with my neighbor, Joe, whose house was adjacent to ours.

Joe was a couple of years older than I was and moved into our neighborhood from the village just after we did. Our families were some of the first settlers in Kamirenda, so just beyond the last houses was the bush. Joe taught me how to make catapults out of old tire rubber, so the two of us and his dog Sasha could go hunting. We didn't need to go very far from home to hunt for birds, mice, rabbits, or even wild antelope.

We set up traps for birds using a sticky glue-like sap that came from a local tree. We smeared the sticky substance on a piece of wire then set the wire up among some high branches or positioned it on some shrubs. We would hide nearby, and as soon as a bird landed, we would run back and catch it. This glue was so strong that the bird's feet would be stuck completely. So as long as we got to the wire before it could fly off, the bird was ours.

We also set traps for mice. We would attach a corn kernel or a peanut to a string inside of an old can of beans and leave the traps overnight. Mice were drawn to the smell inside the can. As soon as it ate the food, the string was released, and the trap would close, shutting the mouse inside for us to find the next morning. Our families loved it when we brought these delicacies home; my mom especially loved to grill the mice.

Every night, we had dinner around seven thirty. If my dad was home, I was promoted to the high table to eat with him and my brothers. The girls ate together and so did the boys. Dinner options included nshima and chicken, nshima and greens, or nshima and dried fish. Nshima was a staple in Zambian meals, especially in our house. My mom or sisters would pour cornmeal into boiling water, stir until it formed a thick porridge, and then shape the cooling dough into small, bread-like lumps. We would use nshima like a utensil to facilitate eating any protein or vegetable by hand.

When my mom would decide to treat the family to one of her chickens (usually a rooster, as hens were saved to lay eggs or make more chickens), I was entrusted with the slaughtering. As long as she knew which chicken was on the chopping block the night before and kept it in the house the following morning, my job was easy enough. But if she chose which chicken we were going to eat after it was already in the yard, then forget about hunting or soccer. My friends would come over and help me chase the chicken half the day until it was tired enough for us to catch.

Overall, our food portions were very small. A whole chicken could feed my family of ten for two days. It wasn't that we weren't hungry enough to eat it all at once, we just didn't have the privilege to eat at will. My mom had to be economical. She planned our meals in advance. When my dad was paid at the end of each month, my mom took a bus to the local markets and bought all kinds of food in bulk. If we ran out of anything before my dad was paid again, she would return to the market to buy only what we needed. Bottles of cooking oil, canisters of salt, and containers of washing detergent would become luxuries. But the local scattered shops called *tuntembas*, would sell oil, salt, detergent, and any other essentials by the spoonful, and that could keep all of the families in the community going in those last few days before payday.

When we didn't have electricity for the first year in the new house, we used our battery-powered radio to listen to local shows after dinner. But after we installed power, we could watch television together instead. We gathered in the living room, listened to the news, and then watched whatever shows were on that day. The most memorable were a South African show called *Egoli*, a British show called *Hammer House of Horror*, and a few American shows like *Hardcastle and McCormick*, *MacGyver*, and *The Fresh Prince of*

Bel-Air. I typically went to bed around ten o'clock at night, listening to my brother as he played some Don Moen gospel music on a cassette.

Luanshya, such a beautiful town, was dying a silent death with every sunset. But at eight years old, I wasn't aware of that yet.

2

Mulligan

An extra shot allowed after a poor shot,
usually after a failed first attempt

$\mathcal{B}$efore my dad lost his job, the leadership at the Luanshya Copper Mines subsidized membership at the local golf club for its employees. All miners were encouraged to participate in some form of exercise, so my dad got a golf membership at Roan Antelope Golf Club and also played in a soccer league.

After he was retrenched from the mine and we moved from the mining compound in Roan to the neighborhood in Kamirenda, my dad maintained his membership at the golf club. This allowed him to make connections with the mining executives and influential business people who hung out there. It wasn't until my dad had gone almost six months without work that one of the executives he had befriended at the club offered him a job. That was the first time my entire family clearly saw the value that golf could bring to our lives.

Once he was working, my dad continued visiting the golf club a couple of times a week. Golf, however, was an expensive game.

He had to pay a fee to play Saturday events. There were caddy and green's fees, and the culture of the game in Zambia almost always involved a few friendly bets. Altogether, a weekend of golf could easily cost a couple hundred kwacha. For a man with eight kids, a partially constructed house, and not a lot of expendable income, it was a lot of money.

My dad had a few work-arounds, so he could maintain his membership and its associated connections. He skipped on betting whenever he was able, and to avoid caddy fees, he had my brother, Sydney, caddy for him for free.

Unlike in other parts of the world, caddying in Zambia was a full-time job that men supported their families with. Because of this, my dad was not particularly well-liked by caddies at Roan Antelope Golf Club, who felt my brother was taking work opportunities from them. When there were more caddies than golfers, which frequently occurred, caddies without a loop either went home or fetched for lost balls in the stream to resell.

One time, Sydney wasn't available when my dad wanted to play a round of golf, so I had the opportunity to caddy for him. Even though I was seven years younger than my brother, I made up for my lack of strength with enthusiasm. I loved the experience so much that my dad let me take over for Sydney, who didn't really enjoy doing it anyway.

My interest in the game was instant. Whenever I saw my dad miss a drive or putt, I envisioned how I would have done it. He typically aimed to the left of where he intended to hit the ball and played with a smooth fade that curved from left to right. But he sometimes curved it too much, resulting in the ball landing well right of where he wanted it. I watched him struggle through an event once and couldn't let go of the thought that I could have done better even though I had never swung a club before. I kept asking my dad if I could try playing, and eventually, he let me hit a few shots in front of a caddy named Ben Kalunga, who watched and gave me pointers.

Once golf entered my life, I didn't necessarily have time to play soccer in the streets or go hunting anymore. I started walking to the golf club after school, spending most of my day there and then waiting for my dad to wrap up, so we could walk home together. Sometimes, we didn't leave until nine or ten o'clock at night. Our house in Kamirenda was about a thirty-minute walk from the golf course. On rare occasions, we'd catch a ride from one of dad's friends; this was how I learned that some cars had air-conditioning, could play music from CDs, and didn't have to be pushed to start. The rest of the time, we walked.

Our route took us through the golf course itself. We would leave the club, walk down the fairway of hole number 8, and then cut through some bushes that let us out about halfway through hole number 7. There were no lights on the course at night, so we walked in the dark without a torch or anything to help us see where we were going. The path we took was entirely based on memory, and even then, I knew it wasn't really safe. Roan Antelope Golf Club had water hazards on fourteen out of the eighteen holes, and the bridges over them were so old that most of their supporting chains had been stolen over the years by scrap metal dealers.

On top of that, my dad usually had a Mosi lager or two in his system before we left. The slight buzz helped him to brave the long walk, and I learned that it made him talk a lot. My dad would tell me long stories as we walked home, stories about my grandmother dating a Greek colonialist, who taught her to drive a car, or about what life was like during the war. And while I did like listening, sometimes his voice sounded too loud. I would worry that he was making us vulnerable to predators hiding in the tall grass. I had heard rumors of armed robbers hiding on the golf course, which scared me just as much as the thought of witches, cats, and owls had earlier in my childhood. On nights when I hadn't gone to the club with my dad, I found that I could never get to sleep until he was home safely. If someone harmed him, I didn't know what would happen to us. That thought lingered at the back of my mind. It always felt like a breath of fresh air when we finished the first half of the journey home, and reached the Welcome to Luanshya junction.

From that point on, we were off the golf course and back to civilization. The second half of the journey home was filled with the smells of people's dinners, the sound of singing, and the twinkling of candlelight as most homes didn't have electricity and were occupied by people who squatted in these unfinished houses.

Our neighborhood had a couple of taverns, so people stayed out late, and we could hear music playing until midnight. While the sights and sounds were familiar as we passed, they scared me in a different way. The unemployment rates in Zambia fluctuated between 40-50 percent, and the majority of people (even those with jobs) were just surviving. As I got a little older, I, unfortunately, noticed how limiting life was around my community. Very few people went beyond high school and then joined the masses patrolling the streets and probably succumbing to the temptation of alcohol or drugs, which seemed to be the draw for many guys I knew.

But maybe golf could be an escape from that future. All of my dad's friends at the golf club were better off. They bought me Fantas and ordered me spring rolls from the kitchen. They had luxury cars and discussed international affairs. I liked hanging out with their children too.

While at the club, I made a friend named Desmond. His mother, Miss Rhoda, was a classic, vibrant Zambian lady. His father, Mike, was a British national that originally came to Zambia as an expatriate to work for the mines but had since transitioned and established a variety of businesses around town. Desmond exposed me to videogames, and his family's servant's quarters were the size of my entire house.

It was a large shift from what I was used to. Up until then, hunting for birds and mice with Joe had felt like the best time of my life. But after seeing how the other half lived, I slowly began to separate from that earlier part of myself.

Competing in my first tournament felt like a great way to move in the direction of this positive future. Desmond and I were both going to participate in the 1997 Chick o' the North junior tournament at Ndola Golf Club. The club in Ndola was forty minutes away by car, and my dad was able to secure me a ride there with Desmond's mom.

The plan was to meet her at the Welcome to Luanshya junction at six o'clock in the morning. The junction was a convenient meeting place as it sat halfway between my house and the road that connected Luanshya to other towns. Many hitchhikers caught rides to Ndola or Kitwe from there. And on the odd night that my dad's friends gave us a ride from the golf club, we would get dropped off there to walk the last fifteen minutes home. (The road beyond the intersection had so many potholes that my dad's friends feared the potential damage to their cars.)

Dad opened the door to my room at five o'clock, switched on the light, and saw that I was wide awake. I hadn't been able to sleep all night; instead, I daydreamed about playing at a new golf course and competing in a tournament. I literally lay in bed with my eyes wide open, counting the seconds until my dad opened the door to my room and told me it was time to get ready. I had drawn water from the well the previous night, and my dad heated it up for my bath.

When it was time to get dressed, my dad went to his bedroom, picked up what was perhaps his tightest-fitting polo shirt, and handed it to me. It looked like a dress on me, but he told me that I had to wear a collared shirt, which I didn't own, as part of golf etiquette. I also learned that I couldn't wear jeans or my regular shoes. These new clothing rules fascinated me. My wardrobe was pretty limited, so in addition to my dad's dress-like polo, I wore my school uniform pants, *tuckees* (or sneakers) that I borrowed from my sister, Josephine, and one of my dad's hats. My dad also sprayed some of his Brut cologne on me for a fresh smell.

After having tea and a couple of slices of dry bread, we were ready to go. My dad walked me the fifteen minutes to the junction. It was a very quiet walk, the only sounds coming with the cool morning breeze was the odd neighborhood rooster and insects from the nearby stream. Unlike during our walks together at night, I could study my dad as we walked in the sunlight. I looked at the tiny black bag he always kept tucked between his elbow and chest and realized at that moment that that must have been a pistol. I wasn't sure if that knowledge made me feel more or less safe about the future walks home from the club together.

We waited at the junction for a couple of minutes, and then Miss Rhoda and Desmond pulled up shortly in their Jeep. I waved goodbye to my dad, and we were on our way. As we drove, Desmond and I ate egg sandwiches that Miss Rhoda had prepared for us. I was content. It was fun driving in a nice car, listening to music, and eating a second breakfast. The only pain point was the conversation. Even though his mother was Zambian, Desmond didn't speak Bemba; he and his mother only spoke in English. This was a skill I was just starting to learn, so our conversation was pretty limited.

I should not have been surprised. At the club, everyone spoke to me in English, including my own dad. Before he and my mom moved to Luanshya, my dad studied for a certificate in English as a foreign language at Kwame Nkrumah College in Kabwe. This was initially a shock because we only spoke Bemba at home. I wasn't any good at English, but I knew that I would need to learn if I wanted to succeed in the club environment.

We arrived at Ndola Golf Club to a very packed parking lot. The Chick o' the North tournament was Zambia's premier junior golf event and attracted kids from across the country. I had never seen so many kids in one place before, and especially not all wearing polo shirts and carrying fancy equipment. There were banners everywhere. Miss Rhoda ushered us to a table marked Registration, and we received participation gifts. The event was sponsored by Colgate-Palmolive, which gave each participant a hamper. Mine had a towel, a toothbrush, assorted sweets, a pen, and a kid's storybook. I was being rewarded just for being there.

After signing us in, Miss Rhoda left us with the tournament administrators, who paired Desmond and me with two other kids, one from Lusaka and one from Ndola. It turned out that they knew each other from Simba International school, and they spoke to each other in fluent English. Desmond fit right in and I kept my distance, often chatting with the caddies whom I most related to. These kids had full sets of golf clubs and stand bags, and they wore bright polo shirts and golf shoes. Up until this time, I didn't know there was a shoe specifically made for golf. And my golf set had been donated to the Roan club, and only included four clubs. I had a 3 wood, a 6 iron, a pitching wedge, and a putter, which all fit inside the red pencil bag my dad had discovered in an unutilized locker. It was clear that my clothes and equipment had room to improve.

We were playing nine holes and happened to be the party right before the top juniors in the country. This meant that, for the first time, I had somewhat of an audience while I played, as some onlookers were waiting to watch the group coming after us. My opening tee shot even drew some applause, regardless of my crooked ten-finger grip and open stance.

After we finished our loop, the event offered a buffet lunch of unfamiliar and delicious food. While I ate and enjoyed the club atmosphere, I saw a satellite television for the first time and, consequently, heard the name Tiger Woods for the first time. Highlights of his Masters win were being played, and the people around me were speaking almost reverently about this golfer. I was captivated by the sharply manicured fairways with their bright green grass displayed on the screen. It was exciting and confusing. Until that point, it didn't really register that there was an actual world outside of Zambia, let alone a world of golf. It was like, suddenly, I was aware of a whole new planet.

All of the day's participants were then ushered to the area where awards were being handed out, and television cameras began to appear. Reporters were there to cover the event and show the prizes being handed out. To nobody's surprise, the overall event was won by Madalitso Muthiya, a fifteen-year-old prodigy dominating golf across the country. He had been a member of the party right behind mine. He won the event by a wide margin.

But to my complete surprise, the name they called for the next award was mine. I was the overall winner in the under-thirteen division. Everybody clapped as I walked to the front to accept my medal. I stared right at the television camera that I saw was aiming directly at me. Maybe my name would be one that people praised while they watched highlights of golf tournaments. I felt a sense of purpose like never before. The atmosphere, the people, and the rush of adrenaline moving through my body was like nothing I had ever experienced.

After the awards were all given out and the presentations were done, a list was read of the upcoming junior golf events in Zambia. The next tournament was scheduled in Lusaka. Even though I knew Lusaka was a few hundred miles away, a boy in my party had been from there, and everyone around me sounded like they were planning on going, so it didn't seem impossible. I was excited to get home and ask my dad if I could go.

On the ride home, Miss Rhoda stopped to grab us dinner at Hungry Lion, probably my first ever takeout meal. My family didn't have a house phone and Dad didn't have a cell phone, so we were not able to let my dad know that we would be arriving later than we had originally arranged to meet him. He must have been waiting a while when we pulled up to the Welcome to Luanshya junction; it was already dark. Miss Rhoda told my dad that she was so proud of how well I played and congratulated me for winning my division. I bid Desmond and his mother farewell and walked home with my dad.

When I began to explain that the next tournament was in Lusaka, my dad cut me short and told me it was too far and cost a lot of money. As a kid, I hadn't started processing the level of commitment and resources required to play in tournaments. That trip to Ndola was an eye-opener. All the kids I played with had pocket money to buy a Fanta after we finished, and I was there looking on and sipping on tap water. While I was disappointed I couldn't travel to the next event, I didn't let that ruin my good mood.

All of my brothers and sisters were waiting to hear about my time in Ndola, and I was more than happy to provide details for them over the course of the next hour. I felt that describing the day's events was almost as enjoyable as experiencing them. I knew then that I had never been a part of something as exciting as that tournament in my entire life.

When we retired to the couch to watch television, the news was on. The reporter was running through the list of top stories of the day that would each have a few minutes throughout the broadcast. Toward the end of the list, I heard the reporter announce that "top junior golfer, Madalitso Muthiya, won the 1997 Chick o' the North golf tournament." I quickly jumped from my seat and knocked on my dad's bedroom door to let him know they were going to show highlights from my event. My whole family waited until the report came and were blown away when the first clip they showed of the tournament was my name being announced and me walking up to collect my prize. Our house was instantly filled with screaming. I was on television!

As I lay in bed that night, I felt renewed and inspired in a very special way. I had a taste of the spotlight and wanted more. Was there a future place for me where I received this kind of attention, where my family and peers admired me? For the first time, I started imagining a future in golf, in the spotlight, and outside of my community.

VINCENT in action.

Young Vincent takes golf by storm

YOUNG Vincent Kabaso has done wonders in the game of golf. At 11 years old today, he has already competed in a major tournament.
    Last year in August he took part in the Chick "O" North tournament in Ndola and won the third position with 76 net.
    He also played at Roan Antelope Golf Club during a fundraising stableford competition and won a second place with 32 points.
    Vincent who is in Grade Six at Luanshya's Mpelembe primary school is son of former Luanshya Division employee Albert Kabaso, also a golfer and is now working for Mpelembe Drilling. They live in Kamirenda township.

First newspaper article at 11 years

3

Head Up

Looking up too early to see a
result, causing a bad shot

*T*he first golf magazine I ever saw was in the locker room of the Roan Antelope Golf Club. As soon as I picked it up, I could tell it had been in there for a while. My guess was that it was maybe twenty years old. The pages were worn and slightly crumpled, and the colors had faded, especially in the corners where many fingers had turned its pages. I picked it up and flipped through it, just to see what was in there. Nothing new, I assumed, and yet, the magazine in itself was new to me. When I was done, I put it back where I found it. It was nice to know that anytime I wanted to thumb through the articles, it would probably still be there.

That was the beginning of a beautiful relationship. A few years later, when the golf course in Luanshya flooded and was unplayable for five months, I considered golf magazines to be my best friends.

Each morning after breakfast, I would pick out around fifteen *Golf World* magazines from the collection I had acquired and then go outside to sit beneath the mango tree we had in the yard to read them. I had a system. First, I went to the back of the magazine to review the winning scores. This section had short articles about recent tournaments that reported all the players who had made the cut and their earnings. Then I'd flip back and forth through the pages, eventually reading all of the feature articles in the order that they interested me. The features usually described new design projects, the opinions of the editors, and any major news stories in the world of golf. I always found myself reading the articles with instructional tips last. They never particularly helped me with my game and were more likely to confuse me than anything else. I was more of a visual, experiential learner than someone who could read about a technique and feel knowledgeable enough to try it.

Up until that time, I hadn't really considered myself much of a reader, but golf magazines engaged me in a way that books never had. Golf had become a staple in my life, and my obsession with the game was only growing.

In 2003, I was invited to play in the National Junior Stroke Play Championship. Part of the prize for the tournament was a spot on the provisional team competing in that year's All-Africa Junior Golf Challenge. It was the first time Zambia was hosting an international junior golf event, which was a big deal for the very keen Zambian audience. The best player under sixteen years old would also win the opportunity to represent Zambia at the British Junior Open. I was very motivated to play well. I finished fourth overall, and as the best under-sixteen player. I was announced as Zambia's representative to the British boy's championship, which preceded the open championship.

Altogether, sixteen players made the provisional team. The best four would get to represent Zambia in the All-Africa Junior Golf Challenge. Mike Bayliss, a South African PGA-trained professional from Zimbabwe, was hired as our coach to prepare the team. He ran a couple of golf sessions with all of us and then trimmed the team down to eight players, sending the rest home. At the final trials, I was elated to find out that I had officially earned a spot as one of the final four on the Zambia National Junior Golf team.

The core team was me, Lester Butts, Alfred Tamba, and Youngson Sinkala. Brian Kabwe was given a wild card and stayed on to be the team's reserve. We would be competing against teams from countries like Zimbabwe, Kenya, Malawi, and South Africa. It was exciting to know that I was going head to head with some of the most prominent names in junior golf at the time, including George Coetzee, Anton Haig, Branden Grace, and Matthew Kent.

In the time leading up to the All-Africa tournament, Mike studied our stances, grips, and swing techniques. He gave us golf magazines to inspire us and keep us focused even when we were not at the club. I became a student of the game like never before, trying to soak in what Mike was teaching me.

The most difficult challenge was my grip. Mike wanted to switch me from a strong grip, meaning my hands were positioned to the right of my club's center, to a more neutral grip, meaning I would need to get used to positioning my hands down the middle. This was a pretty drastic change, and in practices, I was not having as easy a time hitting a consistent draw as I was used to. Mike must have been on to something though because, a week before the tournament started, I recorded my first ever hole-in-one; it was a beautiful 5-iron shot on the third hole of Nchanga Golf Club. Mike was so proud that he treated the entire team to a special lunch.

A few days before the tournament, we got to move into a fancy hotel. It was my first time staying in a hotel and my first time seeing a bathtub; my shower at home didn't have a tub, and due to its low pressure, we typically improvised with a bucket.

The day before the tournament began, Mike pulled me to the side and told me that he had decided to replace me from the starting line up with our alternate, Brian, because he wasn't confident that I could perform consistently with the neutral grip. I was distraught. After making the cut, going through the training, and getting excited to play, the opportunity was being taken away from me at the last minute. To rub salt in the wound, I was forced to give Brian my uniform since they had only planned for four participants. We had a practice session that day, but I was told not to bring my bag.

And at that evening's dinner, Mike said I could go home if I wished, but also reiterated that the guys would love to have me stay. I had not considered going home until he suggested it. My teammates were gracious, and even though it was painful, I ended up staying. I knew that it was better for me to experience an international tournament firsthand as a spectator than to watch it from home on my family's black-and-white Sansui television.

There was a lot of fanfare on the opening day of the tournament. The sports minister of Zambia attended the flag-raising ceremony, and the entire town was drawn to the event. I had never seen so many people interested in watching golf before. I could feel the energy emanating from every corner of the room, but I felt disconnected from it, and the team spirit wasn't as exciting as before the team changes. When it was time to take the official team photo for the newspaper, one of the golf executives asked me to stand to the side because they only wanted the players in the starting lineup featured.

In the end, taking me out of the lineup did not seem to help the team. Zambia finished in the last place. And on top of the fact that the host country's team fared the worst, Brian and Youngson got food poisoning from the previous night's cocktail dinner. Their run back and forth to the nearby bushes for relief during play was highlighted in the local papers' report covering the event.

My father came to see the tournament on the final day, clearly confused to see that I was not teeing off. Once he understood what had happened, he immediately told me to pack my backpack, and we were on our way home. The whole way back, I kept wondering what could have been if I hadn't changed my grip.

It wasn't long after that tournament that our area flooded, and I found myself sitting under that mango tree, reading golf magazines once more. Having gone through an experience like that and not being able to go to the club to practice was hard. The thought of my dream dying just like that and perhaps never being able to pursue a career in golf frightened me. The magazines felt like a lifeline, something I could focus on to stay on the right path. One of my fears was that, if I lost touch with that part of myself, I would have too much time on my hands and eventually become one of those guys who loitered on street corners abusing all kinds of drugs to overcome the hopelessness of our environment. The truth was that my reality was sometimes scary to face, and those magazines provided me a safe haven to continue to dream.

When I thought about golf, it wasn't only about its impact on my life. I loved the sport. Reading those magazines brought me closer to the game and exposed me to parts of the game I hadn't seen before. Even when my home course was in its best shape, lawnmowers were used to cut the greens, and the bunkers were filled with soil. When I saw how beautiful the golf courses in the magazines looked and how cool the golf carts seemed, I couldn't stop imagining what it would feel like to play on courses like that.

My golfing fantasies were typically cut short, however, when I tried to explain them to my dad. His main concern was that my interest in golf meant that I was neglecting my schooling.

After we purchased a satellite dish in 2005, we had access to channels like ESPN, which would broadcast PGA Tour Classics. My dad and I sat and watched together, and I told him how I wanted to pursue a career in professional golf. He bombarded me with questions about how I would make money. I tried showing him the leaderboards with player earnings in my magazines and explaining that if I pursued PGA training like my coach, Mike, I could teach golf and gain enough experience to run a club. His rebuttal was that the people we knew who worked at local courses in Zambia barely made ends meet. He could not fathom that golf could be a profession instead of a hobby. No matter how much I explained how many career paths I could pursue, he was adamant that I should focus on school and get a good education, which, in his defense, was well-intended.

The disconnect between me feeling so passionate about this career path and him looking out for me, for me, felt like he was pushing his own agenda until I understood where he was coming from. As a child, my dad went through a prolonged period of unexplained sickness, which eventually prevented him from continuing school.

His education was cut short after middle school, and he had been hustling to survive ever since. I knew that he didn't want a future like that for his son. I knew that, as a man with traditional values, he felt that my reputation would influence people's perception of me. So he was adamant that my siblings and I focus on school. But for me, especially, he found it hard when I expressed interest in a career in golf, which was not exactly comprehensible to him at the time.

He had experienced firsthand how much weight reputation carried. Well before he met my mother, my dad had a son whose mother was from an opposite tribe, and her family's reputation was not particularly admired in their village. That alone was reason enough to break off the relationship. In Zambia, a family's reputation either earned a household's respect or proved to be a barrier, and those factors are great deciders when it comes to issues for marriage.

Receiving my prize after winning a local tournament

The other reason my dad tried to talk me out of a golf career was that he didn't want to upset my mom. She had a love-hate relationship with the sport. Initially, my mom wasn't thrilled about me going to the golf club and staying there late with my dad. She was worried I wouldn't pick up the best habits and I wasn't going to put much effort into my education. She felt especially responsible for keeping me on track. It took winning a tournament that was sponsored by the local roundtable for my mom to be convinced I might be on to something. The roundtable was so impressed by my play that they sponsored the rest of my primary school education. They paid all of my tuition fees and even bought me new school uniforms. I remember going around to each shop in town with my mom and the representative from the roundtable, trying (and failing) to find size 14 shoes. Since then, my mom started to come around on golf.

For many of the tournaments I played in, prizes came in the form of home goods. By my fourteenth birthday, I had accumulated an assortment: a microwave, a deep fryer, a refrigerator, and carpets to name a few. Most of the time, I would win appliances that we didn't own, and my dad would have me give them to my mom as presents when we came back from the course. She loved it.

But, eventually, the novelty of receiving gifts stopped outweighing my mom's concerns with my staying out late. She, like my dad, only had a ninth-grade education.

They weren't the only ones who tried to dissuade me from my dreams. I was met with strong opposition from many people who encouraged me to go to college, get a job, and then come back to enjoy playing golf as a hobby. To be fair, nobody in Zambia had ever pursued a career in golf and made much of themselves. The few uncertified golf professionals who had played well and shown potential didn't have enough opportunities to play to earn a living. They had to wait for the Zambia Open, which only came once a year. There were really no progressive opportunities for young athletes in Zambia except maybe for soccer players.

So I understood why people said the things they did to me. It just didn't make it any easier. I was beginning to realize that this was a dream I would have to chase alone. I had essentially rebelled against my own parents about where I wanted my life to end up, and with the many outside naysayers I experienced, I wasn't fazed anymore.

4

Bunkers

Challenging situations that golfers need
to navigate to secure a good round

After I graduated from high school, my math results were not necessarily that great, and the local golf course was going through some difficulty staying playable again. Then the Luanshya Copper Mine executives decided to outright cut all subsidized sponsorship to Roan Antelope Golf Club. Over the years, the number of golfers had dwindled from forty to fifty a weekend down to maybe fifteen at most, and the club, by itself, was not sustainable anymore.

The unemployment rates in Zambia had skyrocketed to well over 60 percent, and there were only two colleges offering degrees at the time. Around 5 percent of high school graduates were admitted to a four-year program. All six of my older siblings got into college. I was at home with my younger sister one year after graduating high school, feeling like a loser, waiting for a dream to come true. It seemed like the more I tried to chase it, the farther it got away from me.

In high school

Was I like the other Zambian golf hopefuls who showed so much promise when they entered the game as juniors but hadn't realized how difficult it would be to support themselves as adults?

I had won the Chick o' the North under-thirteen division three years in a row. I made the national team for the All-Africa Junior Golf Challenge five times, and I would have ranked either first or second in the country if ranking points were kept.

After not actually getting to play in 2003, I had become more determined than ever during the 2004 trials. Oliver Seno, a locally based pro golfer from the Philippines, was the coach this time. I had returned to my original grip and old swinging ways and was playing well again.

I was the clear favorite leading up to the qualifying rounds, and I lived up to expectation when I made the team alongside Michael, Mateyo and Suhail. We would be representing Zambia at the 2004 All-Africa Junior Golf Challenge hosted by South Africa.

While we didn't play as well as we wanted, we didn't come in at the last place. We finished sixth, beating only Malawi. But that tournament was a turning point for me, a necessary defeat to help me see the big picture. While the 2003 tournament was technically international, it had occurred in Zambia, and I had been a spectator.

The 2004 tournament took me to South Africa, which allowed me to see a truly international stage. The players we faced were invested, hardworking, and took the competition far more seriously than I had ever seen. Up until that point, my dream had been to become the best golfer in Zambia, but that experience taught me that I could dream much bigger than that.

My dream didn't only grow in terms of what my skillset or title could be, but also in terms of the kind of world I could be a part of. When I arrived in Johannesburg, I was amazed at the number of people I saw walking in every direction, the five-lane highways, and the stoplights. Luanshya had a one-lane highway with no stoplights, and street lights could only be found in the central business area. My mouth hung open in shock over the height of the buildings. In the mornings, I was happy to wake up because I got to go to the breakfast buffet. This was the first time in my life I consistently had access to more food than I could eat.

On the golf course, I felt like the images from my magazines had come to life. There were perfectly manicured terrains at the Benoni Country Club, and players carried clubs I had only seen in the latest press releases. I almost wanted to hide my own clubs, which I wrapped rubber bands around to give them a firmer grip.

There was so much to soak in on this trip. I was a new man when I came home to Zambia, eager for knowledge and excited about the game. I went straight to work: implementing practice goals, developing a training routine for tournaments, and analyzing my performance round by round. I had a thirst for the game that I could not satiate.

That year, I won the Chibuluma Junior Open and I beat Oswald Phiri in the club championship, which he was defending for the fifth time. I also qualified for the Zambia Open. I shot my career lowest score at Roan, a twelve under par (61). With all of my hard work and success, I was not only being compared to Madalitso, the biggest name in Zambian golf who was then playing collegiate golf for the University of New Mexico, but Madalitso himself made the comparison. When he returned to the country to play the Zambia

Open and reporters caught up with him at the airport, he was asked if he knew anybody he thought was taking after him. He said my full name. I was being noticed by my own role models.

I played for Zambia in the All-Africa Junior Golf Challenge four more times. I went to Namibia, back to South Africa, Botswana, and then when I was eighteen (my last year as a junior), we went to the All-Africa Zone 6 championships in Swaziland. I was progressively better each year as I refined my process and committed myself to the game.

Right before graduating from high school, my future looked bright. Then, like fate, a fax message was sent to all the clubs in Zambia that the Golf Union had secured two division 1 scholarships to America that would be awarded to the highest-ranked graduating junior golfers. I knew immediately that one of those scholarships was mine.

This chance helped to further define my growing dream—I was going to study in America like Madalitso and *then* play golf professionally. I began to daydream about how perfectly my high school experience was going to end and how all of my hard work had paid off.

In the year-end reports from the Golf Union, it was announced that I had earned one of the scholarships. I was overjoyed. However, when we followed up to ask how I was going to receive the scholarship, there was no concrete response. As time went on, I became anxious. I was not in a position of control, and my golf career was at the mercy of somebody else. Then, to everyone's surprise, all the hype died, and slowly, the questions went unanswered.

This was all too familiar, reminding me about the first time I had been burned by the Golf Union. Years before when I had the lowest score in the under-sixteen division at the National Junior Stroke Play Championship, I earned the opportunity to represent Zambia at that year's British Boys Amateur Championship in the UK. My family and I didn't realize that, while we were waiting to hear from the union about the logistics for my travel, the tournament happened and the Golf Union sent another player in my place. We didn't know until we saw an article in the paper with the picture of another boy representing the country. My dad had been furious, but the only answer we ever got was that they needed the participant to self-fund the trip.

As time went on with no response from the union, I realized that this scholarship to America was also an empty promise. The Golf Union had failed me again. There I was, at home in Zambia, trying to remember what my dream had been before I added school in the US to the list, and I was unable to practice and keep up with the routine I had developed because of the issues at Roan Antelope Golf Club.

Little by little, my golf game got worse. I still tried to play an event here and there, but I had to scroll well past the middle of leaderboards to find my name. I started to forget what winning felt like and could only watch from the sidelines as my friends and colleagues won opportunities to travel and represent Zambia at international events. The same people who had given me praise about my talent for years were coming home and telling me how awful I was. Even weekend golfers who had never won a tournament in their lives had something to say about my "bad golf game" and would challenge me to matches.

After a year of not knowing what to do and not making any progress, I had to start thinking about what my life could be if I took golf out of the picture. If I didn't go to college, I could be a trader or house builder. Those options were not appealing to me. Alternatively, I could enroll in a two-year trade school to study agriculture. Most of my friends from school and my siblings had all followed that path, so it didn't seem out of the realm of possibilities. I applied to the college in Lusaka, but then I wasn't accepted due to low math scores. I felt so stupid when I received that news, thinking I had thrown my life away, focusing on golf and getting nothing in return. I eventually enrolled in night school with the intention of redoing my grade twelve math exams, so I could get on with my life.

At that point, I was fed up with everything and started playing cards. I had too much time on my hands and not enough to do. Not all of my friends had gone to college, so I aligned myself with those who didn't really have anything else going on in their lives. It was illegal to play cards, so we did so at a nearby bush. In addition to playing cards, they did all kinds of things over there like smoking weed and drinking local brown beer made from fermented cornmeal. I played cards and drank beer, but for some reason, I never found smoking appealing.

Gambling was my main vice, and I wasn't particularly good at it. To sustain the habit, I started selling my prizes one by one until it got to the point where I felt like I had literally given away everything of value I had ever earned. One day, an argument broke out during a game, and I found myself in the middle of a bloody knife fight. That really opened my eyes, and I cut all ties with that group and that lifestyle. I had always been afraid to end up like those guys, and for a while, I had let that nightmare become my reality. How had I let that happen?

I started spending more time at home, asking myself hard questions, and honestly being pretty miserable. Sometimes, I would read books that my brother Albert had by Myles Munroe and Bishop T. D. Jakes. In one book, Jakes talked about how nothing just happens, how pitfalls and struggles are there to challenge us, and how nobody chooses a dream based on the difficulty of the journey along the way but because it was a part of their destiny. This struck a chord with me. My passion was golf, and the road had been difficult, but maybe I hadn't veered too far off the path. Maybe that could still be my future.

Thinking about where things went wrong before, I realized that I had spent too much time relying on other people. I knew now that nobody was coming to save me. I knew that I didn't really want to go to school in Zambia and live an ordinary life. I also knew that my dad could not afford to send me overseas for school. Acquiring a scholarship on my own was the only option.

I didn't have much time, but if there was any left, I was going to use it to try to salvage something, to get back up and fight. I was frustrated and didn't know where to start, but I knew that I needed to get moving forward whatever it took. With this renewed drive, I went back to the golf magazines and immersed myself in them.

One day when I was watching television, I saw a report on Tiger Woods winning the 2005 Masters. As I watched the extended coverage, I had an idea. What if I wrote to each of the reporters mentioned, told them my story, and asked if they could connect me to a US college? Immediately, I wrote a handwritten note about how I was a determined Zambian with aspirations to pursue a career in golf and seeking a scholarship. I addressed the letter to the BBC and threw it into the outgoing mail without a stamp.

Between 2005 and 2007, I wrote thousands of these letters. From Thursday to Sunday, every week, I sat in the living room with a pen and paper, waiting for the three-minute segment of the BBC sports report that covered golf events from the week. I would copy down the names of the reporters, write more letters, walk to the local post office, and follow the same process as my first letter, addressing each envelope to the BBC without a stamp.

I didn't receive a single response until one morning in May 2007, when Anna-Chomba shouted that there was a mailman looking for me outside. They came once a week, ringing their bicycle bells outside any house with a delivery. This particular letter needed my signature. When I opened the envelope, it was from someone named Mr. Robinson from the British PGA. He was letting me know that he'd received my letter and was forwarding it to the Royal & Ancient Golf Club of St. Andrews, which had the capacity to give educational grants. I had learned about the history of the R&A through all my readings, so I knew what kind of opportunity this was. Together with the United States Golf Association (USGA), the R&A helped govern the game of golf worldwide since 1952. The R&A was able to use surplus funds from hosting the Open Championship to support golf development efforts, such as providing grants to student athletes. They were headquartered at the Royal & Ancient Golf Club of St. Andrews in Scotland, which was the oldest and perhaps most famous golf course in the entire world. Even though I had put all of my faith into this process, I didn't really believe that anyone would ever answer me. I was so relieved that something positive was finally happening to me. I could have cried.

A few weeks later, I received a letter from a Ms. White of the Royal & Ancient Golf Club of St. Andrews saying that they would be willing to offer me a grant, but it was dependent on me securing a place of study for the upcoming fall semester at any institution. With the letter, she also sent a booklet of addresses for colleges offering golf programs. The academic year started in August, so I quickly wrote letters to every single school in the booklet.

I only received one response from my letters to universities. It was from a man named Jonathan McDonald, head of Land Based Studies at Cannington Center of Bridgwater & Taunton College in England. He offered me a place but indicated that they did not provide scholarships. We exchanged another round of letters before he suggested that I create an email account to cut down the three-week waiting period between letters.

I was nineteen years old, and I had never used a computer before. With the deadline for securing my enrollment and grant fast approaching, I rushed to the local internet café and had an attendant help me set up my account to send an email to Jonathan. I was shocked to see him reply within minutes. I knew then that this technology would become a game changer for me.

After getting accepted to Bridgwater & Taunton College, the next letter I received was from the Royal & Ancient Golf Club of St. Andrews. They were offering me a partial grant to subsidize my studies. The grant still left us with a £3,000 balance. I told my dad what I was up to, and he said that the balance was too much, especially since his work was having trouble paying salaries. He would sometimes go three months without pay. It bothered me a while, but I knew that this was very likely my only shot. So whatever it took, I could not let the opportunity slip away.

5

Driver

The club used to begin most golf holes,
with the most potential for distance

*I*t was pitch black. Mpongwe, a huge farming area with milling and beef factories, was about a hundred miles behind us on the single-lane gravel road we had been traveling on. The villages we had passed since then did not have electricity, and my truck was dead on the side of the road.

I opened the hood of the beat-up Toyota truck I was borrowing from my dad to check if the problem was something clearly visible, but I couldn't see anything in the dark. I grabbed the security torch my dad had also loaned me and returned to check the engine area. It smelled like burning rubber, but I still didn't see any obvious issue for why the truck had suddenly stopped working. I had zero mechanical experience. One time, I had seen my dad unhook a tube from somewhere under the hood to suck out some petrol, but that was about the only problem I could potentially fix. Unfortunately, I had the highest level of mechanical knowledge in the group, as none of the fish merchants I was transporting knew how to drive a car, let alone fix one.

Kamirenda home with dad's beat up 1970's Toyota truck

We tried many different things for an hour without success, including sucking on a few different tubes. I knew that the car had some issues—the speedometer didn't work; there was no stereo; the brakes jammed sometimes; the fuel level could only be measured by a stick we inserted into the tank; the car didn't start without a push; and previously, the entire engine had been dismantled and pieced back together—but my dad had just had it serviced, and there had been no additional red flags to worry about.

Eventually, we gave up and decided to camp where we were stuck on the side of the road. The four men slept in the open back of the pickup, while the woman and I tried to catch a little sleep in the cab. This was truly the middle of nowhere. From where I was trying to get comfortable in the driver's seat, I could see monkeys in the trees and antelope in the distance. I knew that this area also had much more frightening wild animals, which I was trying not to think about. After the fish merchants had advised me to keep my voice low, just in case, I decided that I was more willing to risk us getting hit by a passing vehicle than to venture a few feet away into the complete darkness to set up warning signs and potentially get mauled to death by who knows what.

This trip wasn't really working out the way I thought it was going to. The plan had been to ferry fish merchants from Mpongwe to the great lakes in Kuchishimu and back over the course of about three days. During warm weather, traders in the fish business would stock up on tilapia, or bream, to sell at the local markets. These markets offered fish (fresh or dry), indigenous fruits, herbal medicines, and second-hand clothing stations. They could typically be found near bus stations, which made them easily accessible to traders traveling with their wares, indigenous people purchasing food and supplies, and travelers looking for a cultural experience.

There was an area where trucks could park as well so that people who needed help transporting larger items could book their services. I had heard about this type of business in passing and figured out that I could charge every passenger as much as fifty dollars to transport them. If there was enough business, I could earn extra money to help pay for school. My dad had done everything he could to help raise the money I needed for Bridgwater, but there was still a fairly large balance that had to be paid before I could go.

Even though my parents hadn't taken me seriously when I started the application process for Bridgwater & Taunton College, once I received the grant from the Royal & Ancient, they realized that my plans were legitimate and tried to help me with the process. Initially, the idea of me going to school in Europe may have seemed too far-fetched to seem real, especially considering that my golf scholarship from the union had not worked out.

I was able to handle everything until I needed to send a deposit to the school to secure my place. The admissions team would not send me the immigration paperwork for my student visa until the deposit was paid. My dad hustled and scrounged around for the money, but he was unable to get anywhere near enough. He ended up selling my grandmother's house, and she moved in with us. Although this was not the full balance of what I owed for the semester, it covered the deposit, guaranteeing my place and allowing the process to continue.

After I processed all documentation for my trip, we had just about exhausted every option to raise money. We still needed to pay for my plane ticket to England, the remaining (though smaller) balance for my classes, as well as my living expenses once I actually got to school. I was hoping that, by shuttling the fish merchants, I could cover these final costs.

My dad sent me off with his truck, the torch, and ropes we could use to tie up the logs of fish in the back. I drove to Kalala Market and parked next to some other trucks. I was approached by a group of fish merchants, four fairly thin men and one plus-sized woman. Three of the men sat in the truck bed as I drove, and one man sat stiffly between the woman and me in the front. It was a tight squeeze, and I had trouble shifting gears the entire way.

Part of the deal was that I had to do this job late at night to avoid traffic officers. The truck I was driving was technically not supposed to be used to conduct business, and I didn't have a driver's license.

The entire trip to Kuchishimu was going to take about nine hours each way. Once we arrived, the plan was to drop three of the men by the harbor to go fishing and for me to camp overnight with the others to wait. Interestingly, I learned that women are not allowed beyond the harbor due to a long-standing cultural covenant. If she went any further, then the whole party risked never being seen again or becoming mentally incapacitated. There was also a rule that we would have to bring gifts to pay homage to the chief, whose blessing we needed before the men could do business in the area. If we failed to do this, the trip would be cursed. So before the fish merchants got into the truck, they bought bread and milk at the market as their offerings.

Once we were on the road, I asked those sitting in front about how their business worked and how long they had been doing it. We chatted most of the way, but after a while, everyone passed out, and my only company was the sound of the gravel road under my tires.

This, however, was short-lived. Right after midnight, we were stopped by a roadblock manned by armed policemen. These men worked with game rangers to control the killing and selling of game meat. We told them we were merely going to a farm, but they still searched the truck. I was sweating bullets, but luckily, the policemen were more concerned about the contents of the vehicle than any other laws being broken. They didn't ask for my license, and they sent us on our way.

Then around two o'clock in the morning, all of a sudden, the headlights of my truck dimmed and then the gas pedal stopped responding. I shifted into neutral gear and tried to jump-start the engine before we came to a stop, but there was no response. The truck was dead, and that's when we spent our first night stranded in the wilderness.

Shortly before six o'clock the next morning, the sun rose. The men in the back of the truck estimated that we were about an hour away from our destination. We didn't have any option except to wait and hope that a car came our way.

The fish merchants had strapped large ice packs to the truck bed to keep the fish fresh for the journey home, and now they were starting to melt. My fear was that whoever ended up helping us would not be able to restart my truck and only be able to offer transportation. The merchants would need to leave without me in order to still have ice left for the trip home. Not only would this scenario leave me stuck in the middle of nowhere with a broken truck by myself, but I also wouldn't get paid for the trip.

Around eight o'clock, we saw an older gentleman on a bicycle. I couldn't speak his language, but the merchants could. They asked him if he knew anyone who might have mechanical experience and where the closest village was. He told them that we were not too far from a village settlement, so one of the men went with him to find us some water and assistance. A few hours later, our man came back with water, and that was it. However, someone told him that a car usually drove by on this road every couple of days. It seemed like that was really our best hope.

That entire day passed, and we didn't see anyone else. We used the bushes to relieve ourselves. The fish merchants bundled the ice in huge sacks to slow down the melting process, but I could feel the sack getting cold as the ice melted anyway. We had not brought any provisions, so we drank the water from the village and ate one of the loaves of bread meant for the chief. At this point, I was pretty sure the trip was already cursed, and I preferred not to go hungry.

The second day went much like the first, until right before sunset when we heard a truck coming in our direction. I stood in the middle of the road and waved my hands to stop it. The driver had been slowing down anyway in order to pass us on the single-lane road, so he pulled over.

Four strong-looking men disembarked and asked us what the issue was. I told them about the lights dimming and everything shutting down. They asked me to open the hood, and one of the men inspected the tube transmitting petrol. He said it was likely that this tube was clogged, and it needed a good blowing. He pulled out the same tube I had tried fixing that first night, blew out some petrol, and then put a bucket underneath the engine. I could see how much dirt was in there. He walked me through the process and after giving the car a little push, *voom*, it came back to life.

I was overjoyed and relieved. The truck was running, the men hadn't charged me for their help, the fish merchants weren't leaving me, and I could still make money on the trip. But there was a small part of me that wished I had been able to fix the issue when it arose and save us from two days of waiting.

When we arrived at the chief's yard around 9 o'clock that evening, we met the assistants who received the gifts on his behalf and gave them the milk as our offering. Because it was too late to continue traveling, we spent a third night in the truck.

The next morning, we walked about ten miles and then boarded a boat made from a huge log. We paddled for an hour. It was a mix of adventure—fun and fear, especially when the boat swerved. But I could tell that the locals knew what they were doing. One was in the front, steering, and the other one was in the back.

We docked then walked another five miles to the harbor. This was where two of the fish merchants (the woman and one of the men) and I would be camping in roofless huts while the remaining members of our group went deep on the lake, with the locals and their boat to spend "a day or two" fishing.

We ended up waiting for three days. Each morning, I went to the harbor and saw other people coming and going. To pass the time, I read a Good News Bible that I had brought with me. We ate fresh fish and wild fruit.

On the morning of the fourth day, I woke up to see a cow's head hanging over the top of my hut. This apparently meant that the fish merchants were back. Due to the weight of the fish, the men used cows to transport them in bundles. They caught most of their fish during the night, using nets, or *ububa*, which was a powderlike substance sprayed on the water that irritates the fish and causes them to float to the surface.

When we loaded the fish onto my truck, the weight made it seem like the truck bed might collapse. I felt sorry for the cows then. Thankfully, we didn't have any issues on the drive home. The entire trip took eight days—eight days of sleeping in a car or on the floor, eight days without a proper shower or meal. By far, this was the hardest-fought $250 I ever made.

The fish merchants wanted me to bring them back to the lake again, but I wasn't doing it. I felt lucky to have survived the first trip, and I wasn't going to risk a second one.

When I got home, I reported my earnings to my family. I think they hoped that, given how long I was gone, I might have been able to complete two or three trips, but I had finished only one. My dad tried to get a loan at the bank, but we didn't have any collateral, so they refused. He also tried going to loan sharks, who had legal licenses to lend money at double the interest, but that didn't work out either. We were running out of time, and we were desperate.

Then one day, my mom opened my bedroom door first thing in the morning. She asked me to get ready and go to the local bank with her. When we got there, she told the teller that she would like to close her savings account. I was in the room when she signed the paperwork to withdraw her entire life savings. The total amounted to about $600. That money bought my plane ticket.

The night before my trip, my entire family sat around our living room table and prayed for me. Beatrice, who was now living back home with her two sons, led the prayer. This was the most united I had ever seen my family. As I looked around the room at my grandmother, my dad, and my mom, I was so thankful for them. I was aware of the extreme lengths they had all gone to, how they had given up everything they could to help me follow my dreams. My family did not typically show affection in verbal or physical ways. I never saw my parents kiss, and we didn't say things like "I'm proud of you" or "I love you." But that night, as we sat there together, I could feel the love they had for me.

On the day I left, I still had no money for living expenses and still owed some money for classes, but I would have to deal with those problems in England. I shed a tear as I left the house, and I could see that my mom was doing the same. My dad didn't cry until he dropped me at the bus stop to Lusaka.

I took a direct British Airways flight from Lusaka to Heathrow, determined to be worthy of all of my family's sacrifices, thrilled to start my grand adventure, and anxious for the challenges that were sure to come.

6

Fairway

Where you hope your tee shot ends up

$\mathcal{W}$hen Jonathan McDonald caught me after class and told me that Marie, the international student liaison officer, wanted to meet with both of us that afternoon, I couldn't tell if my heart began beating so quickly that I couldn't feel it, or if it had stopped beating altogether. Since I had arrived at Bridgwater, hearing the name Marie automatically gave me a sinking feeling in the pit of my stomach irrespective of who said it. I gave Jonathan a tight-lipped nod.

I had been dodging Marie for days. Before I had even left Zambia, she sent me a note, trying to convince me not to come to school if I didn't have the money to pay the full balance for the semester. I ignored this email. A few days previously, she had sent me a message, expressing her alarm that I was here, living on campus, enrolled in classes, and still hadn't paid everything that was owed.

Even though Jonathan and I had a good rapport going, the fact that Marie was involving him, the head of Land Based Studies, in the discussion didn't seem like a good sign. I had only arrived in the

UK three weeks ago. Was that all the time that I was going to get? Was this another dead end for me?

When I arrived in England, I had been in very high spirits. During the ten-hour flight, I watched movies, took a few naps, and read *Your Best Life Now* by Joel Osteen. As we began the descent into Heathrow, I gazed outside at the panorama of twinkling lights shining up at me from London. Based on my experience in South Africa, I thought I knew what I was about to see, but the magnificence while approaching London was one of a kind.

I wished I could've paused time to fully appreciate the sights, but before I knew it, we had landed. However, there was no end to my amazement that evening. Once on the ground, the first big difference I noticed between Zambia and England was the temperature. As soon as I was off the plane, I was hit with a gust of cold air. Zambia's average temperature was about 10 degrees Celsius or 50 degrees Fahrenheit. That Heathrow wind was closer to freezing than I had ever experienced before.

I had instructions to take a train headed to Somerset County where the residence director, Ms. Rutendo, would be waiting for me. Although I was supposed to be looking for that train, I got too distracted by the architecture inside the terminal. I must have lingered a bit too long staring at the ceiling because, the next thing I knew, a helpful airport security guard approached to ask if I was alright. He helped me find my way to the right platform, and soon, I was on a train to Taunton.

As I sank into the cushioned seat, it struck me how strange it was that I had grown up hearing the trumpet of our local steam trains and catching glimpses of the cattle being transported inside the cars as I walked along the tracks, but that I had never actually sat on a passenger train before. Apparently, my inexperience showed. Unbeknownst to me, I had made myself comfortable in the first-class section of the train. I sat there until the man who came to punch my ticket let me know that I belonged in the crowded standard section. I moved in embarrassment.

When I reached Taunton, Ms. Rutendo was easy to find. She

recognized me the moment I got off the train and welcomed me to both Bridgwater & Taunton College and to England. She then ushered me into her blue Ford to drive me to campus.

During the ride, I learned that the school canteen hadn't opened yet, so Ms. Rutendo made a stop to grab me some tea. I told her I wasn't thirsty, but tea ended up meaning a meal. I had a delicious plate of fish and chips on her recommendation.

England seemed to be full of surprises. What I saw out the window during the drive to school was nothing like the London cityscape I had imagined. The Cannington campus of Bridgwater & Taunton College sat in a rural area of Somerset County. This was the farming hub of England and Wales, and well known for its ciders. We drove through very narrow country roads covered in nothing but darkness.

The quiet continued when we arrived on campus. Ms. Rutendo told me that I arrived a week before class registration commenced, which meant that I was the first student to check into the dormitory building.

After a few days of familiarizing myself with my new room and country, I managed to find my way to the golf club where I introduced myself to Ron Macrow, the director of golf. We chatted briefly about playing golf in Zambia and what that was like. Explaining my journey to Ron was an interesting experience. I didn't take ill to the fact that my story was beyond his imagination.

Overall, Ron was excited to have me at Bridgwater. He told me about his hardships, mostly his unsuccessful attempts to recruit elite players to the golf program. I think that my arrival gave him some hope; assuming I worked out well for him, he could have the opportunity to expand his golf program beyond local kids.

In general, golfers like to ask each other about which clubs they use, and Ron wasn't any different. He was surprised when he heard my answers. My dad and I shared one set of golf clubs, an assortment of old makeshift clubs that we had acquired over the years. He was shocked. After I described how I used rubber bands to enhance my grip, Ron asked me if those were the clubs I used when I represented Zambia in international tournaments.

I replied yes, and he seemed impressed. Then I showed him the only equipment I had thought was in good enough condition to bring to school: a used glove that a professional golfer had given me the last time I played in the Zambia Open. After losing interest in the glove, Ron started looking me over. He asked me my shoe size after noticing the tight-fitting flip-flops on my large feet.

"I wear size 15 shoes, sir," I said.

"Please don't call me sir. Call me Ron," he replied. He handed me some paperwork to fill out, which included a section asking for my measurements for shoes and team uniforms. "Boy, we're going have to set you up real quick. We have our first scheduled match coming up in two weeks."

So until classes began, I committed myself entirely to golf. I left for the golf club early in the mornings and stayed there until closing time, using an extra set of clubs that Ron loaned me. It wasn't hard to practice all day, but it did take me a while to work out the time differences. I particularly struggled with the late sunsets. In Zambia, the sun always set at six o'clock in the evening, and that was how I knew the day was about over, so I'd go home to eat. In England, it stayed bright well into the evening. I missed a lot of meals simply because I didn't think it could possibly be close to dinnertime. Luckily, I still had fifty-four pounds leftover from my train ticket. I used this money at the convenience store right outside the student housing to get snacks.

One day, Ron asked me to go down to the video room with him, so we could get my swing on camera and review it together. When he was ready with the camera, I hit a few shots. One of them elicited a huge reaction. Ron threw his arms in the air, cuffed me on the shoulder, and gave me a huge thumbs-up.

"I may have just found that kid I've been looking for in you," he said.

I tried to shrug him off, but he reiterated that he had never seen so much raw talent and was so impressed with how technically fluid my swing looked. I smiled, but if I was being honest, I was quite skeptical about listening to other people's opinions on my swing. The last time someone critiqued my form was in 2003 when Mike Bayliss tweaked my grip, and I would never forget how that turned out. I hoped Ron's comment was genuine, and it seemed like it was when he sent an email to Jonathan (to whom he reported) after our session, expressing how excited he was to have me on the team. After so many years of effort to get myself to this point, it meant everything to hear someone else say what I had been telling myself all along, that I had potential.

While everything was starting to fall into place on the golf front, my financial issues were far from solved. When I left Zambia for the UK, I knew that I needed to find a job as soon as I landed. I figured that between the Royal & Ancient grant and the deposit that I had paid up front, I could put some of the money toward tuition and some toward living expenses. If I lived frugally enough, these funds could get me through the first two months of school. What I earned from my hypothetical job would have to cover the balance of what was left for the semester.

After my first meeting with the finance team, however, they convinced me that it made more sense to use the entirety of my grant money on tuition, which would cover a longer period of time. This meant that I had more money going toward tuition than I had planned and not nearly enough left for living expenses. On top of that, I learned that, before I could work in England, I needed to have a national insurance number. And once I found a job, there was a cap to the number of hours I could work as a full-time student. The reality of the situation was that it was not going to be possible to work my way through college the way I had envisioned. I needed a backup plan.

Option A was my family. I knew that my dad hadn't been paid in four months, but if he got paid, then maybe he could help me with living expenses for a few weeks. I reached out to see what his situation was, and he still hadn't been paid. In an effort to try to borrow money to send me, my dad went back to the bank and the loan sharks. The bank denied him a loan, and the loan sharks wanted the title to our family house in order to do business. As soon as my mom heard, she nipped that plan in the bud. They had no money to send me. My dad had tried his absolute best, but I knew it took a toll on him. At that point, I needed them to go ahead with their lives and let me face the consequences of my decisions alone. Option A was out.

Option B was friends. One member from the Roan Antelope Golf Club had emigrated to England. He visited Zambia a few months before my trip and told me to reach out to him if I needed anything once I was settled. The concept of a brother's keeper was realistic in our culture, so I believed that he was a lifeline I could count on. However, after I explained my situation to him, he didn't offer me any assistance.

My dad also knew some Zambian expats in England. When I reached out to them, they told me that they would rally the Zambian community to raise money for me, which sounded great. But for all of their efforts, in the end, they only sent me twenty-five pounds and then called my dad to shame him for sending me to school without any money.

Option C was begging. I started planning what to write on a sign and thinking about what street I could go stand on. The sign could read "Talented Golfer Looking for Sponsorship." But before I followed through with that option, the residence director, Ms. Rutendo, heard about my predicament. She presented me with a newspaper article all about option D: sperm donation. Even though I knew it wasn't something I should take lightly, I really considered it. I knew I could make more money at the clinic than begging for change on the sidewalk.

Thinking about my options was really upsetting. I had heard so many anecdotes about people who left their countries with nothing except the clothes on their backs or with only twenty dollars in their pockets who worked their way through college and ultimately found success. That had been my dream. But now that I had arrived in a country in that exact scenario only to find that working wasn't a real option, I realized that those stories are bullshit. Finding success when you have no resources or means of income has nothing to do with hard work or heart and everything to do with luck. And I didn't seem to have any.

I started a mantra in my head, "It can't get any worse, it can't get any worse," and that kept me going despite everything that I was dealing with, or at least that kept me going until the moment Jonathan told me that Marie wanted to meet with us both.

That afternoon, I found them waiting for me outside Jonathan's glass office. Marie was a slender French woman whose English came out with a thick French accent. She had dark curly hair and wore the highest heels I had ever seen. Jonathan was 6 foot 2 with a big beard and a heavy Scottish accent. Even though I had spoken with both of them before, today, their accents seemed harder to understand than usual.

Marie started by reviewing all of the agreements I had signed. Then she pulled out a whole folder of emails she had printed out that proved how I understood my financial obligations, and that I had assured her that my dad would be sending me more money. She wore reading glasses that sat low on her nose, which allowed her gaze to flit back and forth between the printed emails and my terrified face.

Then she asked me point blank, "Vincent, how do you plan to pay your tuition fees and live in the UK?"

Searching for an answer, I told her that my dad had put his car up for sale; that my older siblings were putting money together to help me; and that I was looking for a job, so I could start making money. Marie was unsympathetic in her response. She told me that if I reached the end of the existing tuition deposit and couldn't pay anything more, my status as a student would be changed to inactive, and she would be required to report me to immigration services. The authorities, she assured me, would not hesitate to put me on a flight back to Zambia if the money was not paid in full. She asked if I understood what she said, and with tears in my eyes, I told her I did.

Next, Marie asked me if I had a return ticket and whether I planned to spend the winter holidays back in Zambia. It was at this point I realized she didn't fully grasp my situation. I was here because it was the only chance I was ever going to have to create a better life for myself. I spent my days contemplating—begging in the streets and selling my sperm—because those activities seemed better to me than going home to Zambia and giving up on my dream. I came to the UK on a one-way ticket, and the airfare cost my mother her life's savings. So no, I wasn't going to fly to Zambia for Christmas. I would have explained this to Marie, but as soon as I had uttered the syllable, "no," she was already onto her next point.

I understood that she was just doing her job, but after thirty minutes of her exasperated sighs, threats, and condescension, I was doing my best to control myself and behave respectfully. It struck me, however, as I turned away from her, that Jonathan had not said a word throughout the entire meeting. I saw him looking at me, perhaps just wondering what life was like for an average African kid. I don't know how, but I could tell that he had compassion and that he was trying to understand my situation rather than critique it.

Then, abruptly, the meeting ended. I hadn't been kicked out or deported, and I still had time to figure something out. Somehow, I came out of there feeling hopeful.

Marie smiled at me on her way out like she had done me a favor, and I couldn't make myself smile back. As Jonathan ushered me out of his office, he asked me to walk to the canteen with him. When we got there, he introduced me to the food and beverage manager and asked if the kitchen had any openings. The man said he was looking for a dishwasher and hired me on the spot. This was a great win for two reasons. First, I'd finally be bringing in some money. And second, I was allowed to bring home free leftover food, which would be a great way to save money.

Next, Jonathan told me that one of the professors on campus was renting a spare room in his house for fifty pounds a week if I was interested. Staying on campus cost me £119 a week, so this would save me quite a bit. In the span of twenty minutes, Jonathan had done more for me than I had been able to do for myself in three weeks.

I don't think Jonathan realized how much help I needed until he sat in on that finance meeting and heard everything I was up against. And even though he didn't owe me anything, he stepped up and helped me. Suddenly, I wasn't alone anymore. I had a friend and a mentor who wanted me to succeed. It felt like a miracle and made me think of a popular African proverb—*ubuntu,* meaning, "I am because we are; my humanity is tied to yours."

7

The Rough

Where errant shots land if they
aren't executed perfectly

My year at Bridgwater ended on a pretty high note. Academically, I earned an advanced National Certificate in Horticulture. And on the golf front, I had raised my game considerably. As I sat with Jonathan in his office, talking through my options for the following school year, he expressed that the school was hoping for me to stay. However, neither of us was sure if that plan was in my best interest, so we tried to think of some alternative options. This was at the end of May, and time wasn't on our side.

My first thought was that I could turn professional and play the local tours for experience then enter qualifying school. Qualifying school is golf's ultimate test for aspiring professionals. Each year, five thousand plus golfers sign up for a chance to earn playing privileges on golf's major tours. Only the top thirty earn playing rights after various stages; it is considered one of the toughest achievements in professional golf.

During the school year, I had tried out for the Gloucester and

Somerset County team, which was competitive in its own right and represented the west of England at a national level. But I hadn't qualified. Instead, I started playing in the local league run by the area's PGA professionals. Over the course of the year, as I played in the local league, I started seeing progress in my game. I was not particularly ready to jump into qualifying school professionally right away, but I knew that my growth in one year at Bridgwater had been pretty good and that I could continue training outside of a school setting.

While I was at Bridgwater, there were a few different drivers that enabled me to enhance my game. The first was having someone to facilitate weekly practices, organize friendly matches against other local college teams, and act as a sounding board on my golf game. This role was played by Ron, the director of golf. Ron was a classic English guy, always impeccably dressed and sporting oversized glasses. He was a career PGA professional who worshiped the philosophies of the golf icon, Ben Hogan.

Although Ron was technically my coach, I had a hard time letting him coach me. It was easier for me to leverage his expertise in the aspects of the game that I wasn't familiar with—measuring my progress with tools and technology that I wasn't familiar with, gaining advice on how to play in weather conditions I had not been exposed to in Zambia (strong winds, rain, low temperatures)—than to let him alter my style of play. I found that when it came to my grip, my stance, and my swing, I really only trusted myself.

The second driver of my improved skillset was, unexpectedly, my access to YouTube. This platform allowed me to analyze my own golf swing. I recorded my swing in the video room or had someone else tape me while I played on the golf course. Then I compared it to the swings of the top golfers. The level of detail that I was able to glean from this process was unbelievable. I used this method to deconstruct and then rebuild parts of my golf swing.

The technological exposure was night and day. Playing golf in Zambia, the only things that I could rely on when trying to adjust my form were my feel—whether a change made my swing slightly better or worse—and my imagination—whether I was able to consistently maintain the change I was trying to implement. Even though YouTube existed when I was living in Luanshya, I had not heard of it. And if I had, I would have had to pay to use a computer in the local internet café. We didn't even have a telephone in the house, so to have the internet at home would have been an absolute luxury.

The third driver was my unrelenting passion. Bridgwater gave me the opportunity to take complete responsibility for my development. The things I had not been able to control in Zambia that had hindered my ability to practice effectively were now behind me. For the first time, I had unencumbered access to a facility and had the power to look up anything I wanted on the internet. This was an opportunity unlike any I had ever had, and it was up to me to run with it.

The Cannington campus had its own golf course. It was fairly new and relatively flat. Overall, it was a forgiving course; even missed drives found an adjacent fairway. Throughout the year, I tied the course record. I practiced day and night and often continued to play in the dark after the lights from the driving range went out. Campus security eventually knew me and didn't give me any trouble for staying out late. Unlike at home, I felt safe walking the four miles back to Professor Stanley's house each night with the streetlights shining the way.

Having the ability to practice for an unlimited amount of time without having to pick up my own golf balls was unheard of. Back at Roan Antelope Golf Club, we used to have an official driving range, but it had been demarcated into residential plots. After that, we hit old beat-up golf balls down the tenth fairway. I would typically bring forty range balls with me and hire a caddy to run out onto the fairway to collect my golf balls one by one as I hit them. I could only afford about an hour of caddy fees, so I went about two rounds. The conditions we practiced in would be considered an unimaginable safety hazard since the caddy collecting the golf balls usually became an unintentional target. When several golfers were practicing, caddies often got hit by golf balls. This could result in anything from a small bruise to actually needing medical attention.

My passion was something that I didn't think Bridgwater had been fully prepared for. I entered the golf program, assuming there would be a professional set up with a full schedule of events, but there were only the occasional college matches. After I expressed the desire for more playing opportunities, Jonathan helped to create a schedule of events that I could play outside of the friendly matches Ron organized.

It didn't take long for me to notice that the level of enthusiasm and dedication I had for the sport was different than what I saw from my classmates. Most of them were sixteen years old and had recently graduated from high school. It felt like they all had an interest in golf but were not committed to it as a career, which perhaps was normal. On difficult days when playing golf wasn't very fun (like on those with bad weather), it felt like an adult daycare, listening to everyone complain. Their negative talk about things we couldn't control didn't sit well with me. I found myself going about my business and practicing or playing alone in these situations, which I really didn't mind. One day, I attempted to practice in nothing but a light polo, thinking that's what it was going to take to get used to golf in near-zero temperature. A good Samaritan caught me around the seventh hole and really cautioned me about making sure I kept warm enough to avoid pneumonia.

Differences like these were some of the reasons why staying at Bridgwater for another year didn't feel like the best choice for me. I had to think about my end goal and decide whether staying in the program another year would be worth the investment.

Bridgwater had initially been advertised to me as a high-performance institute that developed young golfers into golf professionals or club managers. What I had discovered in attending was that the golf program was in its early stages and not fully developed. Although I had been able to take my game to the next level, I found that I had to create or ask for playing opportunities outside of the program.

On top of that, the majority of the tuition that I was paying for corresponded with a course of study that was not aligned with my goals. I had earned an advanced certificate in horticulture, which prepared students to manage sports fields, gardens, or parks. This wasn't really a targeted program for aspiring golf professionals.

If I was going to struggle and hustle to follow my dream, I wanted to make sure I was doing that in the right place. Earning, owing, and paying money was top of mind for me the entire school year. Marie, from the international office, would send me emails, asking for updates on money coming in from Zambia, and Jonathan would always try to reassure me that the decision to kick me out of school was above her. But this was a source of stress for me regardless.

Some of that stress was alleviated, however, when Jonathan invited me to a meeting with him and Ron a few months into the first semester. At the time, I was making eighty pounds per week as a dishwasher, and I knew that I was not going to earn the money I needed for my outstanding balance. Jonathan told me then that he had written a letter to the Royal & Ancient in Scotland and told them about my predicament. They responded by adding an extra £1,000 to my grant and organizing for me to get fitted for a custom set of TaylorMade golf clubs.

I was speechless. But Jonathan wasn't. He just looked at me and said, in his thick Scottish accent, "Focus on your classes, amigo. We'll find a way for you."

That moment was life-changing. Not only because I needed the money to stay in the UK, but because the lesson I had learned in Zambia after the Golf Union let me down—to only trust what I personally put in motion—was maybe not something I needed to apply to every situation. I started to understand that while I was in control of the choices I made and who I decided to trust, that didn't mean that I was limited to only the opportunities that I could conceive of and accomplish by myself.

I cannot fully explain how much Jonathan helped me, seemingly around the clock. He knew that the Royal & Ancient was following my progress, so he took on the weight of making sure that Bridgwater was a good experience for me. He even facilitated a deal that the college could feature me in their brochure to highlight Bridgwater's international outreach if they would offset some more of my tuition.

Beyond helping me increase my grant money, earning money through brochures and dishwashing, and securing affordable housing, Jonathan also loaned me his extra bicycle to use on my trips to class and the golf club. He also bought me an MP3 player (and recommended some Scottish music I might like), occasionally bought me groceries, and invited me to gatherings in his home. Jonathan had become a father figure to me.

So as we talked through my options for the next year of my life, I had full faith in him and trusted that whatever he recommended would be the right path for me. After I pitched the idea of qualifying school, Jonathan and I looked it up. We realized that, in order to follow that course, I would need to have residency in the UK, which likely wouldn't be feasible. So instead, Jonathan suggested we look at other, more elite golf schools.

He helped me research a few options in both England and his native Scotland. After a few phone interviews, a Skype interview, and an awesome recommendation from Jonathan, I was accepted into Elmwood College in Scotland. I would be earning a higher national diploma in professional golf and also be part of the golf team, which was better organized and had already signed two other international students that year. Part of my tuition would be covered by another Royal & Ancient grant that I applied for, and part would be covered by a charity fund established by a golfer I had played with at Bridgwater. Although I would still need a job in Scotland to pay the balance, I knew that I could handle it.

As I reflected on my year at Bridgwater, I came to the conclusion that challenges are, in fact, opportunities. They are designed to test our abilities, our stamina, and our passion. They weed out those who would give up instead of pivoting and finding another way.

A day or so before I left for Scotland, Jonathan gave me one last parting gift, a check for £2,000. I don't know what I ever did in this life to have deserved the level of friendship, mentorship, and generosity that I received from Jonathan, but as I boarded the plane from Bristol to Edinburgh, I made a promise to myself that I would become worthy of it. It is those "raised by the world" experiences that have inspired my outlook on life.

Jonathan with his wife

8

Tempo

The smooth coordination of movements during a golf swing

*T*he final round of the Elmwood College year-long stroke play tournament was scheduled for a Wednesday afternoon. The standings heading into the tenth and final round were Gary in first; Marc in second; and then a three-way tie for third between me, Ryan, and Martin. I trailed Gary by about three strokes and Marc by one. There were still about thirty students playing, but only the five of us had a realistic chance of winning. Gary's dad had hyped up this series, promising a trophy and a cash voucher to the winner.

Even though a cash prize sounded great to me, it wasn't my sole motivation. Throughout the year, I realized that I had trouble relating to the other guys in my program at Elmwood. They led more privileged lives than me, so it was hard to participate when they were talking about using credit cards to buy gas for their cars or ordering new equipment that I could never afford. Sometimes, those feelings could get me down, but then the golf course somehow had the ability to make us equal. I felt like, as long as the conditions of play were even, then my mind was an advantage. I was stronger than they were because of everything I had endured outside of the golf course. While I may have been at everyone's mercy to get rides or order food, once I stepped onto a golf course, I had my pride. Over the course of the school year at Elmwood, I had gotten comfortable with my swing changes, and I knew that, in this tournament, my talent would do the talking.

All season long, Gary had bragged about how he was going to win. He was a few years older than me, was about my height but with a slightly bigger build, and had a powerful swing. Even though I was skinny, I had my custom-fit TaylorMade clubs from the Royal & Ancient, and I could drive it further than Gary.

Ryan was in form and tried to make a charge through the opening holes. He was a very solid player and had won the Scottish Boys' Championship. When we had drawn each other in a previous match-play tournament earlier that year, it was a very even match. It was a close back-and-forth game for the first nine holes until I got it going on the back nine to beat him. I knew he could come in strong and win on this day. And I didn't underestimate Gary or Marc either.

The course at Elmwood was fairly wide, a little like the course at Bridgwater's Cannington campus. But unlike the very flat terrain at Cannington, Elmwood featured huge undulations on the greens and some near impossible pin placements. Depending on the weather, there could be a three-club difference on any particular hole. Fair weather conditions in Scotland seemed to be few and far between. Some days were so gusty, I couldn't walk in a straight line. On this day, as we played the tenth round of the stroke-play tournament, it was pretty windy, so I knew scores would be high. I just needed to stay patient and avoid careless mistakes.

Overall, Elmwood was definitely a step up from Bridgwater. There were about twenty students in the Higher National Certificate program with me and twenty-five in the advanced national certificate. I was ultimately one of four international students in my program: me, two guys from Spain (Fran and Roberto), and Martin from Germany. The performance program mimicked an American-style curriculum, and this was the first year it was being implemented at Elmwood. While there were some trial and error, each student had a full golf schedule, organized matches, and a personalized performance program.

One of our lecturers, Graeme McDowall, was very dedicated to this project. He was pursuing a PhD in the science of golf performance, and the program was his baby. Graeme was very smart, and I always stayed late to pick his brain whenever he spoke at organized seminars. I was introduced to Graeme when I first arrived in Scotland, after seeing the residence hall with its two-hole golf course and checking in with admissions. He explained the golf program, drove me to the campus' main practice facility (Drumoig), and told me about the planned matches with other schools. I was so excited to hear that many of the guys in the program also had aspirations to play professional golf. I knew this was exactly the environment I wanted to be in.

I was a lot happier, looking at the caliber of players in this program, and I knew that playing with them was a good challenge for me. We played a few matches against university teams from St. Andrews, Abertay, and Dundee. Some guys in my class felt we did not have enough playing opportunities and often participated in events outside of our program. While I would have liked to do this as well, I didn't have the expendable income to do so.

Beyond playing golf, I finally found my passion for golf club management at Elmwood. Classes like finance had never resonated with me before, but suddenly, I could see how they fit with my personality and struck my interest. Though I didn't really consider myself to be a top student academically, I realized that, when I loved the topic of the research or project, it became a lot more fun to apply myself. The more I studied, the more excited I became. It frustrated me to think back to the limited educational system I had growing up.

In the last few months of the school year, I had been working on improving my short game, so it was a little inconsistent going into the tenth round of the stroke play tournament. I had to be strategic about where I landed my shots. I was even par through the fifth hole.

When I got to the seventh hole, I felt confident. I had a history of driving it onto the seventh green pretty easily before. However, this time, I decided to lay up with a 6 iron that went off to the right side of the fairway and left myself a full wedge to the green. The pin was tucked right above the slope on the back left corner. I knew that if I hit it over the green, I was basically dead because there was no way to stop the ball after that. If I missed the ridge in the front of the green, the ball would roll down the slope, leaving a difficult chip shot up to the green. Luckily, I hit a pretty good shot to the middle of the green for a steady par.

I parred the eighth, ninth, and tenth holes with a long 5-iron tee down the middle of the green then two-putted each. On the eleventh hole, I pulled my drive too far left and couldn't find my ball in the rough. I made a double bogey. As I suffered through that drive, I could see Gary playing the adjacent hole.

Up until that moment, I was doing my best to play well while enjoying myself. But once I saw Gary, I began to realize how much this meant to me personally. He was one of my classmates that could afford to play in events outside of school. He had more opportunities to win than I did. And he represented all of my classmates at that moment. Here was a group of guys who had everything I wished I had: they came from the area and knew every street corner, they had support from home and the government, they drove home during the weekends to be with their loved ones, they had their tuitions completely funded, and if they needed, they could tap into other readily available resources. They grew up without ever knowing what it meant to want to play golf but not have a playable course to practice on or to not have the ability to get to a golf course barely thirty minutes away. And over the last two years, I was also frustrated that, in all of these schools, I wasn't just the only African, I was the only black guy. Access to this sport seemed like a privilege that black kids were not afforded regardless of what country I was in.

This tournament felt like my last chance to prove myself at Elmwood. I knew, at this point, that the money was dry. I was not going to be able to continue studying abroad the following year. It was a very emotional thing to come to terms with when I wasn't sure that I was ready to go home. So after the eleventh hole, I let the fire within me start to grow. This tournament wasn't as big a deal to some, but it was to me. And although I didn't know what would come next, I told myself that today I was going to win this.

I was two-over par on the sixteenth hole. It was a drivable par 4, but there were strong winds across the fairway. With my 3 wood, I emulated a shot that I had learned from Tiger Woods on YouTube, the stinger. I played it in the back of my stance and really moved my chest over the ball. It came off like a piercing bullet, never going any higher than fifteen feet off the ground before it landed just on the front edge. I got up and down for a birdie to go back to 1 over par, which I felt was pretty good considering the conditions.

I slipped on the seventeenth as it started drizzling. It was a long par 4 with a slight dogleg to the left. A bogey there put me back up to two over par.

The eighteenth hole was a driver tee shot to a depressed landing that left an uphill iron shot onto the green. I knocked it onto the green in two, and just barely missed the 15-foot birdie putt. I ended with a solid par putting me at 2 over for the day.

Marc was right behind me, so I waited to see him come off before heading to the clubhouse. He birdied the eighteenth hole to finish with an overall score of 76, so I knew I had edged him.

As we entered the club, I learned that it was down to Gary or me to win. He was still playing, so we just had to wait to see what he would do. I heard that he birdied the sixteenth hole, but I wasn't sure where he stood. We sat in the clubhouse with the windows open and saw him par the seventeenth hole. When he came down the eighteenth fairway, he probably thought he had the series won. Given the weather conditions, only a handful of players broke 80.

When he finished, he walked over to where the boys gathered inside and asked what I shot. I told him 72, and he didn't believe me at first. Then he threw his scorecard to the ground, whispered something in one of his friend's ears, and went straight to his car. It turned out he shot a 77. He had a two-shot lead before the round, so the five shots I made up meant I had won the overall series over him by three shots. I never saw Gary again after he drove off, and nothing was ever mentioned about the trophy or cash prize from his dad. It didn't matter to me that I didn't get anything for winning that series; the pride I felt was a prize in itself.

There was some more good news coming. I received a letter that I had officially made the cut to play in the 2009 Royal & Ancient Bursars event at St. Andrews. Overlooking the North Sea, the views around St. Andrews were breathtaking. I walked back and forth across the famous bridge, stood and posed there just as all the great golfers did in pictures and on television. The first round was played on the Eden course before the final round on the Old Course. The Royal & Ancient treated us to dinner inside the historic clubhouse where I was able to admire the priceless art, memorabilia, and trophies from over the years. I was in awe of the entire experience.

Shortly after the day at St. Andrews, it was time to return home to Zambia. Graeme and I made a last-minute attempt to see whether the Royal & Ancient would give me additional money if he designed a special program for me to just compete and not participate in any classes, but it wasn't in line with immigration laws. It was disheartening to come to the end of my time in Scotland, but my visa was expiring, the grant money was spent, and it was time to figure out how these past two years would shape my life moving forward.

Getting ready to tee off at the old course in
St. Andrews Scotland

9

Backswing

The initial move that puts your club in a
position to make a successful swing

$\mathcal{M}$y return to Zambia was not an immediate success.
The first thing I did when I arrived back in Zambia was to contact
Pretoria University in South Africa about formally enrolling in their
PGA program. The Royal & Ancient had suggested I consider this
school, as it was closer to home and less expensive than studying
in the UK. However, once my feet were solidly on the ground in
Zambia, I realized that I was exhausted. It was going to take just as
much effort to raise the money to go to school in South Africa as
it had in the UK. And if I was being honest with myself, that whole
process burnt me out.

I spent the first five months in Zambia living at my parents'
house and feeling as though my advanced horticultural certificate
from Bridgwater and my higher certificate in professional golf from
Elmwood were seemingly worthless. In the ideal version of my life, I
had envisioned that, by the end of my time in the UK, I would have
attracted sponsorship to play golf full time or earned a scholarship

for a PGA school. Neither of those had come to fruition, so I was back in Zambia with no real plan.

What was even more difficult was grappling with my (and everyone else's) false expectation that going to the UK would have automatically set me up for success. In Africa, we viewed someone else's journey to Europe or America as their opportunity to create a life where money is easier to come by. The UK and America represent the epitome of success—the best education, the best technology, and the best opportunities. We expect those traveling abroad to come back, knowing how to continue a successful lifestyle at home.

However, having now experienced two years of struggle, surrounded by wealthy Europeans, I was somewhat stuck between my reality and the pressure from others who assumed I would come back with all the answers. It was tough to explain my new skillset to my dad, and I felt like I was starting from scratch all over again. Finding employment was just as difficult in Zambia as it had been as a nonresident in the UK.

First, I tried to hustle and create job opportunities for myself in Luanshya and nearby towns. I reached out to some golf clubs I thought had the capacity to hire me in a teaching or club management role, but none had the means to pay me. I created school programs and posted them online. I sent the Royal & Ancient proposals to fund golf development initiatives I was creating, but this strategy did not amount to anything. I went to banks and commercial buildings to try and introduce golf to business executives, but I was unsuccessful. I even wrote to golf unions in ten other countries, but nobody had the funding to hire me.

My next move was to try to revive the Roan Antelope Golf Club so that a career there could be a possibility moving forward. At that point, the course at Roan was barely playable. The grass on the greens had grown over six feet tall, and the bunkers had formed into hardpans. A city councilman who owned a John Deere tractor had cut the fairway of the tenth hole so that the fifteen remaining members could use it as a driving range. But beyond that, playing the course was survival of the fittest.

Many members at Roan had died, and many more had been retrenched from the mine and could no longer afford to play. With such a small membership, the caddies had no means to feed their families. Seeing the club where I grew up in this state was heartbreaking.

In an attempt to save the club, I sent a proposal to the office of the district education administrator about introducing golf to schools in Zambia. I also drafted a letter that documented the state of the Roan Antelope Golf Club to the Royal & Ancient, seeking sponsorship for renovations. However, the R&A informed me that they only sponsored clubs that were proposed by golf unions and not individuals. There was nothing I could do.

After not having any success with any of my efforts, I decided to focus on playing golf again. I traveled to Ndola a couple of times a week to get some practice in. I was playing pretty solidly, so I tried out for the national team that would represent Zambia at the 2009 Africa Men's Team Championship hosted in Egypt. It had been four years since I represented Zambia, so when I made the team, I was glad to wear the national colors again. I played well and led the Zambian team to a decent finish. Although I was able to make connections with a few members of the host Golf Union while I was in Egypt, civil unrest broke out in the country shortly after we returned to Zambia, which cut short any plans I had of landing a job there.

At that point, I knew there weren't many other playing opportunities at the amateur level, so I announced my decision to turn professional on January 1, 2010, with the hope of joining the Sunshine Tour in South Africa.

Each morning when I woke up, it felt like I was racing against time. Desperate in my efforts to get my life figured out, I walked to the internet café and spent hours there, looking for a way to make money. I emailed job placement agencies, golf courses in Africa, and golf courses abroad. But even when there seemed to be some interest, the conversations would stall. Most often, I heard back from foreign clubs, but once they understood that I needed them to sponsor my immigration work permit, they would stop responding.

One time, when I looked in the national papers, I found job advertisements for sports administrators, coordinators, and facility managers at the Olympic Sports Council Center that had just been built in Zambia. I thought I had the relevant qualifications and some unique experiences that they would consider valuable, but I didn't even get an interview.

About seven months after I returned home, I received a call from Andreas Scott from the First Quantum Mine. He said my name had come up in a meeting as they discussed sponsoring the next Zambia Open at the Ndola Golf Club. The committee wanted to make some changes to the golf course and hoped to leverage my knowledge of golf course maintenance to prepare the club for the event.

I drove to the club the next day and walked in to an offer. Just when I thought all hope was lost, I landed my first professional job.

The offer was only for six months, but it meant a lot. I continued living at home and would walk to the Welcome to Luanshya junction every morning around five thirty to hitchhike. I needed to be at Ndola Golf Club at seven o'clock, so this gave me an hour of raising my hand to every oncoming car to catch a ride. Sometimes I was lucky and got picked up within minutes, and other times, I'd wait for hours on end.

My daily chores at Ndola focused on course beautification. I worked with a group of guys, cleaning up debris, refilling bunkers, trimming trees, filling animal burrows, and fixing the perpetually clogged pipes. The course was irrigated with sewage water from a local dam, and the water, unfortunately, smelled exactly like what the pipes were used for. I finished work around four o'clock and then got some practice time in before I walked a couple of miles back to the Ndola roundabout. There, I hitchhiked back to Luanshya. I was typically home again at around eight o'clock.

When the day of the Zambia Open arrived, I was very proud. Not only was this an event that I had helped prepare the club for, but it was also my first tournament as a professional golfer. While the event was very successful and my experience was invaluable, my concerns about cutting greens and managing the program were distracting, and I fell a few shots shy of making the cut after the second round.

During the cocktail party that the First Quantum Mine, hosted for the sponsors and players to close the event, I was approached by Mr. Akakandelwa, the general secretary of the Zambia Golf Union. He also happened to be the corporate affairs manager for the Konkola Copper Mines (KCM). He told me that KCM was investing $2 million in the Nchanga golf course, as they had won the bid to host the Zambia Open the following year, and they wanted to redesign their course in preparation. He asked me about my experience working to prepare the golf course at Ndola and about my educational background in the UK. KCM had earmarked an international consultancy company to oversee the redesign of Nchanga, but after our conversation, Mr. Akakandelwa wanted to pitch hiring me as well for the knowledge retention across the two projects. I was ecstatic at the proposal.

It took forever to hear back from Mr. Akakandelwa. Days turned into weeks, weeks turned into months, and still, the budget for the redesign (and my associated employment) had not been approved by KCM. I had confidence that the job at Nchanga would come, but the longer it took, the more anxious I got.

Though I was still working at the Ndola Golf Club after the Zambia Open was over, my contract was only getting extended on a monthly basis. My employment was contingent on whether the club could attract more activity in the wake of the Open. It was initially projected that the buzz from hosting the tournament would attract corporate entities to the club.

However, I knew that the club was not going to aggressively pursue a drive for increased membership for a couple of reasons. First, the highest-paid employee at the club was an accountant who managed the books but wasn't really invested in the game. Second, all committee positions that were invested in the game were volunteers, so the club didn't have a strategic staffer to lead and guide membership initiatives. Third, I was the only person to implement a new initiative (after-work clinics), but it wasn't enough to draw people to the club regularly.

That is when I realized that I was in a precarious position; my job at Ndola was going to end soon, and the opportunity at Nchanga was an unknown. Soon, I would not have any money coming in. To keep myself in the golf community, I needed to come up with a plan that allowed me to continue to travel to Ndola each day and stay relevant.

Just like I had in Luanshya, I started attempting to pitch lessons in Ndola. Because Ndola's economy was driven by multiple sources (unlike Luanshya where everyone's success was tied to the copper mine), there was a more affluent populace ready to hear me. The members at Ndola owned many of the retail, automotive, industrial, tech, and manufacturing companies. If I needed to find a new source of income, these golfers had some to spare. I spent my days advertising group golf lessons for children to parents and teachers at the local schools. I hand-delivered letters that offered individual golf lessons to business executives of the local banks. I pitched individual lessons for adults to current Ndola members, as well as to parents of junior golfers who wanted training to prepare their children for tournaments. I had to be very strategic in my approach as many people weren't accustomed to the idea of golf lessons, let alone paying for the service.

A few kids signed up for clinics, and I soon had it rolling. During the week, I arrived at Ndola around eight o'clock in the morning, played a round, and then ran clinics between three and six o'clock in the afternoon. I structured an individual payment plan for each parent that would keep my cash flow coming at different times to ensure I was never completely broke.

In addition to the group clinics, I also had six junior golfers sign up for private lessons. I held the lessons on Saturday and Sunday mornings before I played in club events in the afternoon. I designed individualized programs for all six of them in preparation for the national team trials. The juniors started getter better, and after five months of hard work, three of the six made the junior national team. I found that teaching came naturally to me, and I was excited to wake up every morning to introduce the game to players at all levels.

Word started going around about the programs I was running, and members began to solicit my advice on questions they had on their form or the rules. This notoriety kept building, and soon, I was fielding questions from the committee that ran the Ndola Golf Club about tournament formats and how to run events. I had the confidence of the executives, and I was able to earn some extra money marshaling and scoring club events.

By the time Andreas Scott called to let me know that the Ndola Golf Club had not implemented sustainable ways to generate income and was cutting my salary from the budget, I was ready.

Soon, I received a phone call from Mr. Phiri, the director of Junior Golf, who asked to meet with me and see the work I was doing at Ndola. He had heard about my drive to introduce kids to golf, which impressed him enough that he offered me the opportunity to be the traveling team manager and coach for the junior team that was prepping for a tri-nations trip to Zimbabwe. He told me that, pending my performance, he would recommend me to the national team in the same capacity. Knowing what was at stake, I made sure that I was available to all the team members, and I did my absolute best to get to know everyone on a personal level. Understanding them as a person helped me bring out the best in them. Zambia narrowly lost to Zimbabwe in the matches, but I left a good enough impression to become the traveling team manager for the Zambia National Team for five assignments.

This period brought a new level of respect for me, and I knew it was only possible because I worked hard to create opportunities for myself. Even when I didn't have a long-term plan, I pushed myself to stay relevant, which was why my name came up in conversations that led to new opportunities. In hindsight, I could have held my breath and waited for the role with KCM at Nchanga to come to me. But if I hadn't implemented my clinics and lessons, I never would have had the opportunity to coach the national team or validate my name in the golfing circles. Like I had learned over and over again, while it is important to put things into action on your own, being proactive saved me, and I realized how many opportunities you can create for yourself by building the right relationships.

Ten months from our initial conversation, I received a phone call from Mr. Akakandelwa, inviting me to meet with the team of experts who had won the bid to renovate the Nchanga golf course. A little over a month after that, I was formally employed by KCM as a sports administrator attached to the Nchanga Golf Club redevelopment project, which brought a lot of action and activity to the local community.

10

Posture

How you address a shot before hitting the ball

*O*n Labor Day, I waited outside of the golf shop of the Nchanga Golf Club as a thirty-seater Rosa bus pulled up. While I was primarily trusted to plan golf tournaments and implement new activities for the club, many of the members and staff were confused when I initially explained my idea for today's event. I noticed some people lingering around the entrance of the club to see what would happen.

The doors of the bus opened, and I could hear singing. Slowly, thirty children from the Mutende orphanage began to disembark, their joyful voices ringing out. The entire staff of the club, as well as many of its members, were quickly drawn out by the commotion and not only joined me in front of the building but began singing too. As the children began the famous hymn in vernacular, even I couldn't hold back anymore.

Demonstrating a trick shot to orphans and
street kids who attended the clinic

Lunch time with participants

We sang, "Bonse aba mupokelela balipelwa maka yakuba bana."
This means "all who have received him, have been given power to be
called his children". Emotion hung thick in the air, and I could tell that
this was going to be a very moving day. After the last song finished,
a quiet mood settled on the crowd. I used this time to usher the
orphans through the clubhouse and onto the driving range where
I had set up an assortment of donated equipment. The bus pulled
away to get the next group of children.

While I wasn't exactly sure what I was doing, I was convinced that hosting these kids at the golf club was the right thing to do. I wanted to provide them with a day of fun, where they could spend time outside and forget their troubles for a while.

The desire to give back was something I had been harboring for a long time. I always did my best to accomplish my goals on my own, but I also knew that I wouldn't have amounted to much if the people in my life hadn't gone out of their way to help me on my journey. The idea of being able to pay it forward and helping someone else's dream become a reality was very appealing to me.

In the past, my ability to help others had been limited. My first memory of wanting to help someone else was when I was eleven years old. I had just started playing golf and was sitting in the clubhouse at Roan Antelope Golf Club when I heard men shouting abuse at a caddy who had walked a few steps into the building. The way everyone was yelling insults, I assumed that this man had stolen something. But when I asked someone what had happened, I was told that the caddy had dared to walk inside the clubhouse where only "important people" were allowed to be. Was that club member more important than the caddy? Was I? I didn't think so. I felt confused and was almost brought to tears as I watched the man retreat from the clubhouse. I could see that he wanted to respond but knew that he may risk his source of income by doing so.

Outside, next to the entrance, there were two large signs, one that said, "No dogs allowed," and another that said, "No caddies allowed." The signs looked so old, they must have been placed during colonist times when discrimination was the norm, but was the value of this man reduced to that of a dog? The whole scene bothered me so much that I went outside and gave the caddy my food from the buffet. Though I wasn't changing much in the grand scheme of things; that was the moment I began my quiet crusade to help those who were considered lesser or felt that they didn't belong.

Once my job was secured at the Nchanga Golf Club to help them prepare for the Zambia Open, I moved out of my parents' house to Chingola. KCM put me up at a local hotel for three months while

I got acquainted with the area and looked for a place to live. One of the things I noticed as I familiarized myself with the town was a small population of street kids. I could find these kids standing outside of stores like ShopRite, begging for change from sunrise to sunset. They slept under bridges and didn't seem to own anything more than the clothes on their backs.

At that point, I didn't have much to give, and I needed to focus on my new job. Energy was high at work, and the club was splurging on renovations: a new first-of-its-kind automated irrigation system, new bunkers, reshaping the greens, and making adjustments to the fairways. This multimillion-dollar facelift brought a lot of hope to a community that didn't have a lot of faith in our mineral resources investors. KCM was actually creating work and business opportunities for local entrepreneurs beyond the distant donations.

A substantial amount of the money was also being committed to the junior golf development at Nchanga. Given my background in coaching and traveling with the junior national team, I presented a proposal to take on this responsibility in addition to my role of prepping the course for the Open. This elated the executive. I went straight to work, promoting free lessons that I taught every Saturday morning to identify potential elite players. Very quickly, the Nchanga Junior Golf Academy became the most happening golf program in the nation. I felt like I had found a career I was passionate about—training the next generation of golfers.

Participants demonstrating dance moves during a break

Street kids warming up before their first golf experience

I was invested and committed to creating a group of high-performance junior golfers. I introduced fitness components into my students' routines and created detailed progression plans that measured my students' development over time that allowed them to compare themselves to elite junior golfers in South Africa. My efforts were so well appreciated, and the junior's program was growing so quickly. As the official golf ambassador of the town, I was nominated to be featured on a huge billboard placed at the entrance of the town to attract new members to the club.

From there, I was asked to help brainstorm ways that we could expand the club's offerings to appeal to local miners. We organized an aggressive recruitment campaign, which resulted in forty new adult members to the club. I lobbied for a budget to buy subsidized golf sets that removed the barrier of recruiting new members without clubs, and I came up with a "one-club, two-hole" event that we hosted on Friday nights that was followed by a complimentary barbeque (or braai). The club president was so impressed with my efforts that when the sitting club manager retired, he promoted me to be the general manager of the Nchanga Golf Club. It was a great experience overseeing the daily operations and attending to membership needs.

When the Zambia Open arrived, I felt very proud. Just like the previous year at the Ndola Golf Club, I facilitated another successful event. In terms of my personal game, while I did participate, I had a decent first round but missed the cut. I was not playing much golf at that point. I had accepted that running Nchanga and its programs were probably the best and highest point of my career. When I thought about my original aspirations of pursuing PGA training, I wasn't thinking much about it anymore. I liked my new role, and it still allowed me to leverage my skills as a golfer to earn a living.

As I settled into a routine in Chingola and my programs were proving successful, I started befriending some of the street kids I passed whenever I ran errands. They were all different ages, but the oldest couldn't have been more than fourteen years old. I wanted to find out what their stories were. Initially, I just spoke with them, but eventually, I started taking them out to eat at restaurants and buying them shoes. I enjoyed our time together though I felt sad when they hesitated to enter stores that I tried to take them in. Shop owners were always quick to throw them out if I wasn't accompanying them. But once they understood that they were allowed to stay inside, the boys would be so happy that they didn't mind the fact that the shop owner was profiling them based on a social status they couldn't control. The unabashed happiness these children felt, just being in a store, reminded me of the joy I used to have when I would go hunting with my neighbor Joe, back when I didn't understand or even care about the world outside of my own.

Once these kids felt more comfortable with me, they started to share their backgrounds. After Luke's father died, he had been beaten by the uncle, who inherited his dad's house and business. After both of Jimmy's parents died, he moved in with his blind grandmother and had to beg for money to buy food whenever the church wasn't able to drop off meals for them. Marvin's father married a woman who regularly beat him with a cane, so he preferred to live on the street. Katai was raised by his grandmother, and after she passed, he didn't have anywhere else to go. Their stories were awful, yet these young boys described their situations with ease. They put on brave faces, but I knew they were hurting inside. I felt terrible that I couldn't do more than occasionally give them food and clothing.

My biggest concern was that these kids would grow up into adults who were still begging on the street without any idea how to support themselves. In a few years, they might have to resort to criminal means for survival. In order to help mitigate the risk of that happening, I tried to offer them advice whenever I could and volunteered at schools to talk with at-risk children about their futures. I felt a strong obligation to share these experiences.

I felt like these kids existed in a reality where they were seen but not heard. They cried out in a silent voice that the upper class did not care to hear. And even though I didn't know how I could personally change the way the street kids were treated, I embraced the idea of trying. So when Labor Day rolled around a few months later, I presented my boss with a proposal to give free golf lessons to thirty orphans and twenty street kids. She didn't really understand why I would want to do it, but she approved my budget.

I wanted those kids to experience a day of love, joy, laughter, and food. I got a local restaurant to prepare packed meals, extended an invitation to the Mutende orphanage, and then rallied the street kids.

When the bus driver returned from his trip to ShopRite with the twenty street kids, I couldn't help but compare them to the kids from the orphanage who had shown up clean and singing. Not one of the street kids had shoes on, they all desperately needed haircuts, and their clothes were either torn or covered in patches. This was definitely not the clientele that Nchanga was used to.

Watching these kids interact with one another and enjoy themselves really made me appreciate the work I did. And selfishly, it also made me thankful for my own family. I picked up a little girl named Naomi, whose mother died giving birth to her and who had nobody else to take her in. There was a set of twins with the same story. I was told that another girl, who was all smiles that day, had been brought to the orphanage after being found dumped on the side of the road. These kids had the most heartbreaking stories, but on this day, they were just like any other group of children who were laughing, dancing, and learning to play golf for the first time.

An hour or so into the free lesson, the juniors that I taught on Saturdays showed up, bringing a new level of energy and excitement with them. It was great to see kids from two different worlds interacting together, and even better to see the street kids and orphans experiencing the freedom and safety of belonging.

We went through the basics of the game; they took turns hitting shots, and then we took a tour of the golf course. Nchanga had hundreds of monkeys around the golf course, which made the experience that much more fun for these kids. This golf clinic was one of the most fun lessons I had ever given, and I knew it would always be one of the most fulfilling things I would ever get the chance to do. I realized how we are all connected—*ubuntu*—seeing the best in each of us and looking for what connects and not what divides us.

The last stop on the tour was the hall of the clubhouse where we all ate together. At the table, one boy told me that he felt like, today, he was part of a family with brothers and sisters, similar to the home he grew up in before both his parents had died. That statement alone made me feel like the day had been worth it.

As I loaded the kids back onto the bus, I felt like the day had done more for me than it did for them. It reminded me that there is a strong relationship between happiness and freedom. When these kids were free from their everyday challenges and free to express themselves without fear of rejection, it was evident how happy they were. Moving forward, I knew that I wanted to continue granting happiness to those that most deserved it and least expected it. That experience will live with me forever, and I constantly pray for how those kids end up.

11

Approach Shot

Your best attempt to reach a hole in the appropriate amount of shots

After finding my stride at the Nchanga golf course, my dream of becoming a PGA professional had faded into the background. My career journey was now fulfilling in new and unexpected ways: I developed junior programs, established initiatives to grow and maintain membership at the club, and I facilitated golf events. My dad had retired from his second job and was still scrambling to get his separation pay, so together with my brothers and sisters, I was able to use a bit of my salary to help support my parents. I had a decent footing in Chingola, and life was good. I was traveling as the coach to the Zambia National Team and was happy with my role.

I was even on the receiving list of an email from the KCM company CEO, Jeyakumar Janaakaraj, or JJ, thanking us for all of the work we had done to transform the golf club. This email was very humbling to receive, as JJ was an important executive and managed the relationships the mining company had with its stakeholders, including the government. It felt like validation for my efforts.

While I was on this high, the vice president of human resources at KCM, Mr. Kaunda, asked me to introduce him to golf. We practiced around his schedule, either early in the morning or late at night. Mr. Kaunda was responsible for approving all new hires and signed our paychecks. One day he asked me if there was anything he could do for me. I immediately responded that I would appreciate it if he could help me to renew my contract at Nchanga. My two-year contract at the club was coming to an end, and I was hoping to stay there for the long term. He said that my request was more than reasonable and that he would do his best and get back to me.

I was excited by the stability that a permanent offer could bring, and that motivated me as I went through my daily routine. While my responsibilities at the golf course varied day to day, most mornings, I stopped in at the mining office to check for scores and updates across the different golf websites on the computer. Having access to golf news and live updates was a game changer for me, and it helped me to be better informed as we made decisions at the club.

One morning as I googled the term "PGA Tour" to take me to the PGA Tour website, I noticed a link for a page on the PGA America website with the caption, "Pathways to Become a PGA Golf Professional." Without thinking, I clicked on the link and saw that there were only twenty universities in the US that offered professional golf management training. The training cost $40,000 a year, and it took four years to complete. I also read that the PGA had nearly 27,000 members, but less than 1 percent of those were minorities. I knew very well that Zambia had not yet produced a PGA professional, and I felt a sense of longing that I had not experienced in quite some time.

Everything about my career was settling into place in Chingola, but at that moment, I started to wonder if the life I had was everything I wanted. Had I reached the apex of my career? Was I living to my fullest potential? Why did I click on that link? I was twenty-five years old with a clear future at Nchanga Golf Club, so why was there now an unsettling feeling that I wanted something more?

Later that night in my apartment, I dug up some of the letters I had written to myself before I had been accepted to a school in the UK. Reading how passionate my words were ignited all kinds of thoughts in my mind. I knew that if I was being honest with myself, the desire to be a PGA professional had never really gone away. Whenever I saw golf on television, I wanted to live in that reality, but I felt as though my dream had likely passed. I had convinced myself that I had explored every avenue in pursuing that career, and I was trying to become comfortable with this alternative path.

For the next week, the desire to pursue a school in America never left my mind. I tried to push it away and focus on what I was doing, but eventually, I cracked. I drafted an email application and sent an edited version to all twenty of the schools in the US that offered the professional golf management program. My entire world felt like it shifted 180 degrees. I was suddenly so immersed in the possibility that my latent dream could come true that I felt like it already had.

Within hours of sending the emails, I started receiving responses from different universities. The first was from the University of Colorado in Colorado Springs, and the next was from the University of Nevada, Las Vegas. In the end, I received emails with invitations to apply from all but a couple of schools. I was shortly consumed by this process and began following through. I went through a third-party evaluation company to translate my prior education to the American equivalent. I knew in my heart that I was not turning back.

On a Saturday morning a few months later, I called my parents and told them that I needed to speak with them in person. They expressed to me that they had plans, my mom was going to church and my dad had a golf game with his friends, but I insisted. Before I hung up, I could tell by the tone in my mom's voice that she was anxious. Typically, when a meeting like this is called, it's to inform elders about one's intention to get married. I was pretty sure this was what they thought I was coming over to tell them. I was afraid that, as soon as I hung up, my mom was going to start preparing a chicken and setting out the plates that she never let us use in order to impress my none-existent fiancée. And even though I wanted to manage her and my dad's expectations, I knew that I wanted to convey what I had to say in person.

Before I got in the car to make the drive from Chingola to Luanshya, I called my older brother, Albert, to tell him the news. I thought it would be less intimidating to tell my parents if I could confide in him first. After he picked up, I told him that I was planning to leave Zambia to pursue my PGA ambition in America. Albert's first reaction was concern. He knew all too well the stress my previous attempt to follow my dreams in the UK had brought to both me and our family. But Albert was sort of the spiritual backbone of our family, and after listening some more, he said that if I was sure, then God would see me through. As I fretted about how my parents were going to take the news, I hoped he was right.

When I arrived at my parents' house, they were waiting for me in the living room. My dad was lying back on the couch next to the door, which he had propped open to let some cool air inside. My mom sat on the other couch, and I pulled out a chair from the dinner table.

"Ndeleka enchito," I said. *I am resigning from work.*

My mom's mouth hung open as she quickly turned and stared at my dad. "Namumfwa efyo alanda?" she asked him. *Have you heard what he just said?*

He slowly repositioned himself so that he was sitting upright. "Do you have another job?" he asked me.

"No, I don't. I'm going to America," I responded.

I could tell that this answer was not what he expected. He asked, "What's in America?"

"I am going to America to study and play golf."

"Do you have sponsorship?"

"Partly," I said.

I watched my parents' expressions. With the scarcity of jobs in Zambia, I knew that my role at Nchanga was nothing to scoff at. The position I held represented both security and comfort. They didn't want me to risk my livelihood to chase a dream.

"Where do you plan to live? What's your plan, and what are you going to study?" my dad asked.

"The trip is supposed to be in August. I intend to study economics, but I am going to be in the professional golf management program, which will make me a PGA professional," I responded.

Unimpressed with my answer, he asked, "Then what? You must be out of your mind!"

He tried to give me examples of friends he had whose relatives struggled to afford life in America. He said that this trip would only make sense if I didn't have anything else going for me, but I did.

When I tried to express that I wanted to be a PGA professional, my mom interrupted me. "What does that even mean?!"

"This opportunity would actually make me the first PGA member from Zambia. So opportunities would be endless," I said.

My dad was still unconvinced, and my mom folded her arms in the traditional African way, as she let Dad continue the interrogation.

"Vincent," he started, "why would you leave a well-paying job and go to America? Are you that misinformed that you'd risk what you have for something you don't even know?"

"Vinny, listen to your dad," my mom added. "We spent so many sleepless nights when you were in England, wondering whether they'd send you back. Why would you want to go through the same? Please listen and stay. There is nothing wrong with the job you have."

Then the room was quiet for a couple of minutes. I could see the fear all over their faces. My mom went into the kitchen and came back with boiled corn, but nobody really felt like eating. After a few more minutes, my mom decided that she was going to church after all.

Dad knew there was no coming back from my decision, so he stood up as well and spoke his favorite phrase, "Anyway, the choice is yours."

The moment after they both left, the power went out on a

scheduled load shedding. Even though this happened frequently, suddenly being left in the dark instilled some fear in me. My trip to Luanshya was more of a courtesy call than a mission to get advice, but after the conversation with my parents, I was starting to understand the real risk involved with my decision.

About a month before I told my parents, I narrowed down the schools I was considering to two: Methodist University in Fayetteville, North Carolina, and the University of Nevada in Las Vegas. But when the Methodist offered me a partial scholarship, a work-study opportunity on the golf course, and a coaching role with the golf team, I had made my decision. It helped that Methodist was also the reigning Division III men's NCAA national champions.

I submitted my formal application and found out within a week that I was accepted. The very next day, I received a letter from Mr. Kaunda at Nchanga that read, "It is my pleasure to offer you permanent Senior Staff employment at KCM. Your dedication and commitment to the company makes you a valuable asset." The permanent offer came with an increase in pay, and it put a stamp of assurance on my career at Nchanga. If I stayed, I would never have to hustle to find a job ever again. I could have the stability that my parents had always dreamed of for me.

I knew that I didn't really have the money to go to Methodist regardless of scholarships and work programs they had in place. But the pride I felt in earning a spot at a college in America and finally being admitted to PGA training outweighed logic. Following my passion wasn't about logic. I felt strongly in my heart that I was meant to pursue a PGA training, and the permanent job offer almost felt like a test of my will. After overanalyzing and agonizing over the decision, I decided to accept the offer from Methodist.

When I returned home to my one-bedroom apartment in Chingola after the conversation with my parents, I looked back at my choice and realized not just how risky but how personal the decision was. I felt confused and conflicted all over again. I tried to reason with myself that having a dream that wasn't aligned with the expectations of people around me was always going to be hard.

What sense would it make if everyone agreed or supported my ambitions? If my parents had been so easily accepting of my dream, then it probably wouldn't have been much of a dream to start with. But no matter who was right, I started to second-guess my choice. In my daily prayers, I started to ask God to guide me through the process.

I thought that before officially deciding to resign, I should seek guidance from some of the club executives. First, I asked the club president at the time, Mr. Zgambo, to meet with me. When I arrived, he could sense that I had something serious to say, so he made sure we had some privacy and tried to calm me down before I began to talk. I told him that I wanted to seek his guidance as somebody I respected and that I had just simultaneously been offered a permanent contract and a spot at a US school that would allow me to pursue my dream of becoming a member of the PGA. To my surprise, he said that he had always thought I would move onto something bigger. He encouraged me to pursue my dreams and recommended that I major in economics.

The next person I sought out was Mr. Nkhuwa, the former president of the Zambia Golf Union. Mr. Nkhuwa's comments were more in line with what my parents had said. He wanted to make sure that I understood I was giving up a great job, and in its place, I would be pursuing a certification without a clear future.

The two meetings didn't offer a definitive answer for me, so I asked Mr. Nkhuwa if he could set up a meeting with JJ, the chief executive. Maybe there was a compromise here. I thought that I could ask the mine to sponsor my education; if they could pay the balance of my tuition and hold my position at Nchanga, then I would return after my studies as a better qualified and more experienced golf professional.

However, just a few days later, an official email was sent to all staff members announcing JJ's imminent separation from the mine. This email caught everyone by surprise. It was almost inconceivable that it would happen, but JJ and his family were relocating to Australia where he was taking up another chief executive role.

When I reached out to him directly, he said that although he was in full support of my decision to study in America, he didn't think it was viable for the mine to sponsor me. If I decided to leave Zambia, I would have to resign.

At this time, I had invested around $5,000 in the admissions process. In order to pay the initial deposit for Methodist and procure a visa, I had sold all of my household goods and pulled out the money I had invested in a friend's company. The rest of the funds for school would come from my partial scholarship, the money I would earn through the work-study program, and (in large part) from my uncle, whose contracting business was doing well in the mines.

The only things left to do were to purchase my plane ticket and officially tender my resignation. I wrote my resignation letter one night, and I asked God to send me a sign that this was the right decision. I vowed that I would not leave the house the next day unless I received this sign.

The next morning, I was literally expecting a miracle. I sat around anxiously, trying to interpret everything I did or saw as a sign leading me one way or the other. But nothing seemed to really jump out at me. By midmorning, I felt like I was losing my mind. So when the phone rang and JJ asked if I could bring a mechanic to his house to look at a lawnmower that had broken down, I was relieved to break my self-imposed quarantine but also a little disappointed, thinking that my demands before God didn't mean much after all.

I picked up the mechanic and took him to JJ's house. While the mechanic was looking at the lawnmower, JJ called me inside. He asked me if I had come to a final decision on whether I would go to Methodist or stay at Nchanga Golf Club. I told him that I was likely going to America. JJ's five-year-old son, Steve, who had been one of the children I coached, entered the room and wanted to show me a new video game he had. I was looking at Steve's game when JJ said that he and his wife wanted to thank me for loving their son and being his coach and his friend.

It was my pleasure to coach their son, and I told JJ so. He called his wife into the room, took her hand, and said that the two of them had been praying for me the previous night. I nodded my head, thinking this was very kind, and he then told me that if I decided to go to America, they would like to buy my plane ticket.

Over the course of my life, I had heard stories of good fortune and of being in the right place at the right time. After having spent all day waiting for a sign from the heavens to tell me that I should continue pursuing my dream, JJ's offer to buy my ticket was the miracle that confirmed my decision. I felt a sense of disbelief and pure gratitude. Here was my miracle—God meeting me through JJ at my exact point of need. This happened on Thursday, and I was on a flight to America the next Monday.

12

Impact

The moment when the club strikes the ball

*W*hen I arrived in the land of the free and the home of the brave, I felt extremely fortunate. Finally, I was in the only country on Earth where anybody with any background could become anything. Caddies become lawyers, trash collectors become business owners, and I was going to become a PGA professional.

In most of the other countries I had lived in, I didn't have the right connections, and so my options were limited. The former Ugandan dictator, Idi Amin, put it best when he said, "There is freedom of speech, but freedom after speech is not guaranteed." In many cases, hard work, discipline, and dedication didn't equal success. My father was a smart, hardworking man, but he didn't quite get his big break his entire career. The last company he worked for, went into liquidation, and nobody got a severance package.

As I settled into life at Methodist, I felt like I belonged. My height and obscenely large shoe size—things I had always stood out for, inconvenienced my mom with, and thought were health problems—were instantly normalized in the US. There were other people over six feet tall, and I met students who wore size 16 shoes. On the golf front, I easily passed my playing ability test, got through to the quarterfinals of the college match play, and I liked my chances to shoot a low score at the campus golf course.

The course itself was like nothing I had ever experienced. The narrow greens had a lot of thick rough around them, and the routing forced you to think strategically about every tee shot. This was wildly different from the courses in the UK and Zambia, which had flat greens and mostly wide-open fairways.

I had been at Methodist for a few months when I opened an email from Jonathan, asking how things were going and if I had a girlfriend. At twenty-five, I was quite a few years older than the other freshmen in my classes. I thought It would have been a little awkward to be talking to nineteen-year-olds. Jonathan jokingly responded to my email, saying I shouldn't contact him again until I had been on a date. I laughed it off, but on second thought, I saw great a sense in his email, so I decided to set up an account on Christian mingle. I was on there for a week when I was pinged with a smile by this girl.

With Hannah

We exchanged a few emails. Hannah told me about her time as an active duty air force officer and everything it involved. We shared a strong spiritual foundation, and we both came out passionate about our beliefs. From emailing, we moved to texting, and then over Thanksgiving break, we spoke on the phone for the first time. Because I knew her career was in the air force, I was half expecting to hear an intense, authoritative voice on the other end of the phone. (This wasn't the case.) That first phone call lasted for hours in her soft Minnesota accent, but it felt like minutes. We told each other stories from our childhoods, discussed holiday plans. She was on the academy tennis team, so she knew exactly what it was like to be an athlete and an aspiring professional.

But it was only a few months after my arrival that international copper prices dropped, and all hell broke loose. The limited demand for copper forced the mines in Zambia to start retrenching workers. The mine couldn't pay contractors, so my uncle (who was paying my tuition) was not able to service his loans or pay his employees. Eventually, the bank was forced to seize his operating equipment.

While this turn of events probably meant that my job at Nchanga may not have been as safe as it had seemed, it did not give me any comfort. I now owed Methodist about $20,000 for the one semester I was there. My uncle wired me $5,000, and then I was on my own.

After my uncle sent what he could, I reached out to Abel, whom I had met from a distant family friend. Abel sort of became a mentor and helped me adjust to life in America. We spoke every day and connected on so many fronts. He had worked at a golf course while in college and was a great support system. I was based in North Carolina; Abel lived in Maryland. When I told him about my predicament, he invited me to visit him, so we could discuss my situation. This was the first time I was meeting Abel in person, but it felt like I've known him for a long time. I hopped on an overnight Greyhound bus one weekend, which reminded me of those trips to Lusaka. We spoke Bemba, made nshima, and shared stories about Zambia, and more.

It was helpful to get advice from someone with a different

perspective. Abel seemed to have a way of saying profound things with ease. He asked me why I was so hung up on the situation at Methodist working out. If I was already in America, he said, that itself was a milestone. Just because Methodist might not be feasible didn't mean there wasn't an opportunity there.

"Don't even think about going back to Zambia just yet," he encouraged me.

We spent the evening discussing all my options. If everything fell apart, we resolved that he would help me get a driver's license. The plan was to look into becoming a taxi driver in Maryland. This would allow me to save some money for a while before returning to my golf dream. Although this goal didn't really align with my plans, it helped me to start thinking outside the box.

The next resource I turned to was Methodist itself. The professional golf management program staff members were resourceful, but they were not able to find a way to help me finance my education. I could not apply for FAFSA without being a US citizen, and I was confronted with the same obstacle when looking into other forms of loans, grants, or relief resources. I even sat down with the college president to see if he could do anything about my situation, but he couldn't. Money talked, and I did not have it. When all efforts failed, it was officially time to leave Methodist University.

When my financial issues began, I was somewhat reluctant to tell Hannah; we hadn't been seeing each other long enough, I thought. But I had been really falling for her, and so I decided to take a risk and tell her everything. She listened to my frustrations and told me that I should do everything I could to continue to pursue my dream, whatever that might look like. As I figured out my next steps, Hannah was a constant source of encouragement. I called her whenever I needed to, and she encouraged me and constantly asked to pray with me.

Before I left Methodist, there was one last option I pursued. I drafted a résumé, logged onto the PGA of America website, and applied to every single job opening that was posted. I sent at least thirty applications. From golf shop assistants to locker room attendant, caddie, or golf instructor, if it was on the job board, I sent my résumé. My attempt was to still pursue PGA training as an apprentice, which, in hindsight, was really the best and most suitable option for me. As one of the two pathways to PGA membership, the apprenticeship route would allow me to work and earn money as I trained, compared to spending $40,000 dollars a year in college.

After a week, I heard back from the head professional at New Haven Country Club in Connecticut, Bill Wallis. I had applied to New Haven's posting for a locker room attendant, but when he saw my résumé, Bill was very interested in my story and past experience working with kids. He was willing to take a chance on me. However, as a nonresident of America, I would need a work permit to accept his offer. He told me he'd guide me through the process, and the many lawyers who belonged to his country club helped us along. After a few phone calls and consultations about the work permit process, we submitted the necessary documents.

The work permit process took as long as six months, so Methodist offered me the option of working on the campus golf course to offset some of the money I owed. Not feeling like I had much of a choice, I agreed.

I picked up pine cones, cut trees, cleared brush, and collected trash on the same course I had just been playing weeks before. When my former classmates practiced, I drove past them in either a Cushman golf cart loaded with waste or on the back of a tractor filled with sand. The fact that the situation was temporary helped to ease some of the frustration. I couldn't fully shake the annoyance that came from the sense of entitlement, some of the students around me had. The idea that someone would have to drop out of college against their will was something many couldn't fathom when they spoke with me.

But these same students were also usually not sure how much their education cost, let alone mine as an international student and a noncitizen. Many of them didn't know where the business office was located because all of their tuition payments were transferred directly from their parents to the school. They didn't have to focus on the financials, and instead, they could prioritize classwork and enjoying themselves. I knew that this privilege wasn't their fault, but when I had the choice, I preferred to smile and wave from a distance and just try to escape my situation.

In Luanshya, my hometown with a population of almost two hundred thousand, there wasn't a single public service law office. My entire country had a handful of four-year colleges at the time, and even the best grades in the world wouldn't grant someone admission if they couldn't secure one of the limited government bursaries to pay for it. And if that wasn't enough, the colleges didn't have Wi-Fi. It was a scramble to access books in the libraries. I had friends who were in medical school who shared one booklet for the entire classroom. These were the facts that I wanted to share when people at Methodist couldn't believe what was happening to me. I had grown up facing the most difficult odds and losing over and over again. But I was still going. And my time at Methodist was just another small part of my story.

One Sunday when I was getting ready to go to church, I realized that I had torn a hole in my only pair of shoes. This was the one time I laughed at my situation. I decided to take a picture of that shoe to serve as a reminder of what rock bottom felt like.

The most difficult question I asked myself was why did I focus so much energy on Methodist, knowing that four years of tuition would be hard to come by? And why did my path take me there? Eventually, I realized that the reason God sent me to North Carolina was to meet Hannah. So many times, life does not seem to make sense at the moment we experience obstacles and predicaments. It is when we look back that the picture becomes clearer, and this experience was such for me.

When it became clear to me that Hannah would love me even at my lowest point, I knew that I wanted her in my life all the time. I took a bus from Fayetteville to Goldsboro and surprised her on her doorstep down on one knee with a ring in my hand. Amid all the uncertainties, this was the one thing I was sure about.

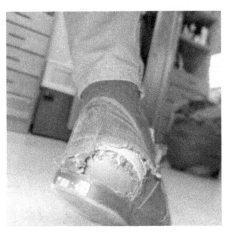

Broken shoe while at Methodist University

"Do you have something to ask me?" she teased with a huge grin on her face.

"Will you marry me?" I blurted out.

"Yes!" she responded!

It was the best response to a question I had ever heard. Our courtship was fairly short, and our engagement wasn't any longer. I proposed on a Thursday, and a few weeks later, we were in the courthouse in Goldsboro, exchanging rings. I didn't want to make the big move to Connecticut and leave any uncertainties about our relationship, knowing beyond a doubt she was the one I wanted to spend my life with. It was a typical Vincent decision, like deciding to move to America and leave everything behind. There has always been a part of me that is willing to take a chance if I strongly believe in something.

Hannah came from a suburban town in Minnesota, and I came from a small African country, which made our relationship atypical. But perhaps this was the fun part, we joked. Our common ground was our faith. She noticed that my faith seemed "extreme," and that I wasn't afraid to dream big and put God to the test. She loved to hear stories of how God had come through for me in the past and about the many miracles I had seen in my lifetime. In a way, this inspired her to deepen her relationship with God. She wanted to make a greater impact on her work and service, and so she asked Him for big things in return.

While I took a detour from my original plan of staying at Methodist, I walked away from the experience with the greatest miracle of all, my wife.

Of course, it wasn't all a happy ending, leaving North Carolina. Debt collectors kept calling me, threatening me with a lawsuit if I didn't pay my Methodist balance of $14,750 in full. There was no running from this.

13

Pure

A well-struck shot, primarily used as a verb

*A*fter Hannah and I were married, I took her on an unforgettable trip to Africa to meet my family and see where I came from. Because my family wasn't able to travel to the US for our wedding, we would be holding a celebration ceremony that Hannah and I dubbed our third wedding—the first was the courthouse, the second was a reception with around three hundred of Hannah's family and friends in Minnesota, and now Zambia with many of my family.

We had a less than ideal arrival at Lusaka; we missed our connecting flight in Johannesburg, and then when we were finally landing the next day, the pilot misjudged the runway and had to pull back up after touching the ground. Thankfully, the second attempt worked out alright. We quickly forgot about this. Immediately upon landing, we were greeted by my younger sister, Anna-Chomba, and my friends. Together, we explored Lusaka and traveled to Chaminuka on a guided safari tour. Hannah led the way as we walked cheetahs, fed elephants, rode a pontoon (which gave me flashbacks of the fish merchants in Kuchishimu), and saw just about every kind of wildlife imaginable. This was a trip of a lifetime for her. We spent a few nights in Lusaka before taking the Wada Chovu bus from Lusaka to Luanshya, the same ride that I had taken when I first came home from the UK. Hannah wanted that same experience.

We arrived at my parents' house for the ultimate treat. My family had prepared a traditional feast for Hannah. They made her nshima and all kinds of indigenous foods. It was so nice to see how easily she integrated and connected with my family. I knew that the monthly letters she had been writing to my mother gave her a strong foundation before our arrival.

Petting cheetahs in Zambia

After a clinic at Nchanga golf club

Over the next few days, Hannah experienced what life was truly like in Africa. She interacted with a few girls from my neighborhood, who found her hair intriguing, and they played with it all day long. She found out what it was like to not have power as we experienced load shedding, and she got cooking tips from my mom on the brazier. She was surprised at the stark divide between races and economic classes, which she observed in town and at the golf course. Even though I had expressed these inequalities before, it was very impactful for Hannah to see them firsthand. She says it helped her understand why I was so passionate about helping people from this community.

Hannah cooking nshima on a brazier during
load shedding (power outage)

I drew so much satisfaction from supporting charities and causes that helped the disadvantaged people from Zambian communities. Most recently, I had donated a about a thousand dollars to various feeding programs being run by well-wishers in Zambia. When I was speaking with the gentleman facilitating the initiative, I realized, "Why don't I do this myself? Why can't I establish a nonprofit and design it to my own vision?"

I had given resources to many different causes and individuals over the years. Whether that was in the form of a hot meal, a pair of shoes, or supporting a golf event, I had given a few thousand dollars to organizations that touched my heart. Maybe there was a way to give back that aligned more clearly with my values and dreams.

Since I had started working at New Haven Country Club, I felt that I had a little more stability, and I could help such causes without bankrupting myself. My role paid okay, but the club also provided lodging for me, which cushioned me, especially as I was making contributions to the debt collectors. As the last of the four assistant professionals to arrive; however, I did find myself living in the garage of the house with no heating. I was simply happy to be there.

New Haven was a great beginning to my career success. I settled in quickly, immediately registered back into the PGA program, and learned the ins and outs of providing service at a premier country club in America. The golf course sat on a beautiful landscape not too far from Yale University, and the membership was outstanding.

Many of NHCC's members were lawyers, doctors, and business executives, who were extremely generous and kind. I enjoyed hearing about their experiences and getting their perspectives on my journey. Many were fascinated with my story. Overall, during my time at New Haven, I helped to double the number of kids participating in junior golf camps, and I launched the women's beginner program. The women in that program had such a good time and reminded me of the real fun in playing golf. It was from this group that someone made me my first-ever birthday cake. That was truly a special moment for me.

On Sunday nights, I liked driving around the backroads near the golf course, reminiscing on how far I had come and taking time to appreciate everything I had. One beautiful fall night, classics by Kenny G. and Don Williams accompanied me on a long, peaceful drive through the misty landscape. Earlier that day, I had received a text message from Ben Kalunga, my father's long-time caddy at Roan Antelope Golf Club. He asked me for help to get his son into college. As I thought about this all too familiar predicament, I suddenly had an epiphany. The charitable foundation I wanted to create could support the educational goals of young people in Zambia. I would name it, Raised by the World Foundation.

The concept was simple. In my own journey, it was all kinds of people that came through for me. Just like ubuntu, Raised by the World represented the best of humanity and how we are interdependent. I wanted to give students the means to pursue their dreams and be the benefactor that I always wished for when I was younger.

Ben Kalunga and Oswald Mulaba with his
family after scholarship offer

So when Hannah and I were in Africa, I hosted a clinic at Nchanga Golf Club to award the inaugural Raised by the World scholarship recipients. The first recipient was Ben Kalunga Jr., whose dad had inspired this idea in the first place. Ben had just completed high school and graduated at the top of his class. However, because his father was a caddy who made, at most, fifty dollars a month, he could not afford to go to college. I knew that if Ben could get an education, we could break the long-standing cycle of poverty for that family. I spoke about this vision and how we might be on to something, I called Ben to the front and presented him with a certificate of support. He was entering an engineering school. I also made myself available to him as a mentor and assured him of my support.

The other recipient we awarded was Oswald Mulaba. I met Oswald when I was living in Chingola and working at Nchanga Golf Club. He was about ten years old at the time when I caught him and his friends trespassing on the golf course as a shortcut to get to their compound on the other side. Instead of kicking them out, I invited the group of kids in for a free lesson to see if any of them would take to golf. Oswald showed a lot of potential. His disadvantage was the environment he came from. His single mother supported her children by trading at the local market. She would often come home at the end of the day without making a sale. Her entire supply of merchandize was not worth more than a hundred dollars, and there was no way she could afford the education her son needed. That day, I informed Oswald that the foundation would cover his tuition at a private high school to give him a better chance at success.

Talking with both of the young men and knowing that I was playing a role in improving their futures meant everything to me. I thought about Jonathan McDonald, who had been (and still was) my mentor and friend, and I knew that he was who I wanted to be for Ben and Oswald.

When Hannah and I returned to the US, we had a very busy couple of years. I left the New Haven Country Club in Connecticut for the Berkshire Country Club in Pennsylvania, which put us a lot closer to each other, as she was now stationed in New Jersey. I passed level 1 of the PGA training, then I took an opportunity to work in sales with Roger Cleveland Golf Company. Although I wasn't sure that I wanted to transition out of the traditional golf club environment, this job allowed me to finally move in with my wife.

Time with Hannah ended up being limited, however. Not long after we started living together, she received military orders to deploy to the Middle East.

When she was gone, I tried to keep busy, so I didn't spend all of my time worrying. I got through level 2 of PGA training and signed up for level 3, the final level, shortly thereafter. I traveled more for work and took up a more competitive golf schedule. I was invited to participate in the annual Rhobarch invitational, which is a charity pro-am event that benefits cancer research in the Pennsylvania area. The event attracted golf professionals from across the state and beyond. It was one of those days where everything just felt right. In the end, our team total of 17 under par got us the win, and my two eagles and five birdies were good enough to earn me the low professional title. I was constantly brainstorming ways to expand upon the Raised by the World Foundation. The scholarships for Ben and Oswald were self-funded, but I knew that I wanted to have a larger impact and help more students. It just wasn't practical at the time.

I had another idea. Maybe I could recruit more people to help. There was no reason that the act of giving back had to feel like a burden that I carried alone. When I thought about what I had needed growing up in Zambia, I came up with two things: money to pay for my education and a mentor to point me in the right direction. If my foundation could not be purely based on giving scholarships, then it needed to address mentorship at a larger scale.

I developed a mentorship program that connected current college students in Zambia to young people in the local communities. The mentors would hold sessions every weekend over the course of a month in their assigned community. During those sessions, they would ask kids to identify potential dreams and ambitions, help them to turn those dreams into clear goals, and then guide them as they developed action plans to achieve those goals. And to keep the kids interested, every session included a meal and a gift to take home. The lessons about what it takes to get into college and how to choose a career were not traditionally taught in schools or discussed at home, so the foundation could bridge that gap and give the youth of Zambia another option. Quickly, the foundation was impacting thousands of children instead of only two.

Even though I was not a PGA professional yet, still had debts from failed attempts at pursuing my own dreams, and was not wealthy by any means, I woke up every morning filled with purpose and gratitude for the works we were doing to positively impact the world. Sometimes, it only takes a small act, a kind word, a plane ticket, some golf clubs, or an idea to change someone's life. I had experienced this myself, and I hoped that my actions would inspire more and more people to pay it forward.

14

Hole-in-One

Almost akin to a miracle, this
is the best shot in golf

*T*here were two ways to become a PGA professional. The first was to earn a four-year degree in professional golf management from one of the twenty accredited schools in the United States. The other way was the apprenticeship route. In order to enroll, you had to have a job at a golf club (or in the golf industry). Then you had to complete three levels of training, each of which consisted of attending a seminar, completing a work experience portfolio, and passing a series of knowledge tests. You had seven years to finish the program once enrolled.

After I left Methodist, the only path available to me was to pursue the apprenticeship option. I honestly didn't mind making the transition as it gave me more control over my success. I liked being able to set my own study schedule and to plan the trips to attend the seminars in Port St. Lucie, Florida. During the seminars, I was surrounded by like-minded people with whom I could network.

Part of me felt like I enjoyed the seminars more than anyone else, simply because of the battles I had waged to get there. I strongly believed that nobody else I met would be standing there if they had to go through what I had endured. This thought gave me even greater pride to be called a PGA apprentice, and this pride helped me realize that I was now thankful to have gone through the struggles in my life. Now I had developed qualities to be thankful for—resilience, persistence, ambition, empathy, and determination. It helped that I had a pretty good golf game too.

Over the years, I have seen deliberate efforts by the PGA to make the game more inclusive. I think the landscape will look much more different in the next ten years. Even from the time I initially started training, I can see a difference.

As a Zambian, I couldn't ignore the fact that I didn't see any black people around the country clubs I worked in. At the seminars too, I didn't see anyone that looked like me. This got me wondering whether the social divides were the same as Zambia and if that contributed to the lack of minorities in these seemingly affluent setups.

I had gotten used to being the only black guy in a pool of hundreds of students from my time at school in England, Scotland, and now the US. While it was no different when I showed up to the PGA seminars, golf tournaments, or meetings, I felt different now. I stood out in the best way. At the seminars and PGA meetings, I was the Zambian in the bright green blazer covered in pins from his international travels. I was somebody who people wanted to talk to. At the tournaments, I was the ever-smiling guy whose golf ball driving distance had no match. And with my financial woes behind me, I was no longer the foreign student who couldn't keep up with school payments.

As people got to know me and heard my story, they were fascinated. The most common question was how I got into golf in the first place. Many assumed that I hadn't picked up the sport until I arrived in America. They were even more intrigued to learn that I had come to America specifically for PGA training. I educated them about golf in my country, and about the world-class designs of the golf courses in Zambia, how those courses could host major events if economics were different. I shared a story of a time I played a browns golf course. This is a golf course with no water system in sight. Some greenery is seen around the rainy season, and cattle are used to graze the fairways in place of a lawnmower. The greens are a mixture of oil and sand, and you scraped your line of play before hitting. Miss the first putt, and the next one was a gimme. Everyone liked my punch line, "You see, for a long time in my life, I never really had a three-putt."

After I passed levels 1 and 2, the crowd of apprentices attending the seminars got smaller. Level 1 had over two hundred attendees, but by the time I got to level 3, there could not have been more than fifty of us. While the thinning herd may have been partially attributed to the seven years allowed to get through the program, I think that the intensity of the workload weeded out those not committed enough.

My final work experience portfolio focused on the operations of running a private country club, and it took me a few months before I was ready to submit. Once that was complete, I passed five out of six knowledge tests, and so I only had one test left to take.

The week leading up to this test seemed to be full of miracles. Days before my test, Hannah surprised me with the biggest news of all: I was going to be a dad. She had entered the house after work with an Allen Edmonds shoe box nonchalantly in her hands, immediately capturing my attention. I followed her like a puppy from the kitchen to the bedroom, ready for my present. When she handed me the box, it seemed unusually light, but my excitement didn't leave any time to think. I ripped the lid off and saw that there wasn't a pair of size 15 shoes, but a pair of baby shoes inside. There was an instant flash before my eyes. I felt like I might pass out as I started to understand what Hannah was trying to tell me.

She grabbed my hand, saying, "You're going to be a father."

"Are you serious?" I exclaimed in disbelief.

I gave her that "Don't play with me" kind of look, but she remained calm and nodded her head in affirmation. That news made the last level 3 knowledge test seem even more important than ever, and it helped to ground me for a greater purpose as I continued studying that week.

Then the day before the final test, I made the last payment on my student loans at Methodist. It had taken me three and a half years of working extra hours and saving every spare cent to send to the debt collectors. What a sense of pride I felt to have paid every bit of that bill (nearly $15,000). The weight of my financial burden being suddenly lifted off my shoulders further convinced me that everything in my life was falling into place. There was no way I wasn't going to pass this test.

On the morning of the test, I ate a light breakfast and reviewed my notes once more. I stopped to smile at the picture of Hannah's ultrasound hanging on the fridge, setting the tone for the day. I got into my Srixon work van and drove to the testing center. Once I pulled into the parking lot, I found myself fighting back tears, thinking about myself as a ten-year-old with a set of hodgepodge starter clubs and regular sneakers, telling everyone I was going to be a professional golfer before I even knew what that really meant. And now, here I was sitting in the car, separated from becoming a PGA golf professional by only one test. I said a quick prayer, took a deep breath, and walked into the building.

Once inside, the proctor, Maggie, looked up from her desk and smiled. I had taken all of the previous PGA knowledge tests in the same center. She had become a fan of my story. She checked me in and had me put my belongings in the provided lockers; they were strict and didn't let you walk in with anything but a calculator and pencil. The revisions I had stayed up all night practicing were playing on repeat inside my head.

"Are you ready to make history?" she asked, knowing that this was the final test before I might become the first PGA professional from Zambia.

"This is it!" I responded.

I walked into the strictly guarded room and eyed the camera that sat over my computer. Even though the atmosphere was cold, as I started the test, I felt strangely comfortable. It felt like déjà vu; the questions looked familiar, and I could tell that all of my preparation had paid off.

I was allocated ninety minutes, but I found myself answering the last question with twenty minutes to spare. I spent that time double-checking my answers to make sure I hadn't made any silly mistakes. Then it was time to click the button and get my score.

When I took my previous tests, I had been amazed that the score appeared instantly, but now I knew the drill and was ready to know if I passed or not. The computer screen blinked a couple of times as it calculated my score and I closed my eyes. When I opened them again, I saw the word CONGRATULATIONS in large bold print and my score of 85 percent underneath.

I was speechless for a moment. I felt like Chris Gardner in the movie *Pursuit of Happyness*, who seemingly couldn't catch a break until the final day of his internship when he was offered the job, or like Vince Papale in *Invincible* when he walked onto the Philadelphia Eagles' field during open tryouts. Even though I knew deep down that I was good enough and that I could succeed, seeing the passing score on the screen still felt deeply satisfying. I threw my arms up in triumph and thanked God. Dreams really do happen if you don't relent, I exhaled. After twenty years in the making, I had finally accomplished my dream. I had really done it, conquered the mountain in a fearless way. I walked out and sat on the steps of the building, shaking and overcome with emotion.

At that moment, on the steps, I realized that my crazy journey was all worth it. The hard work and sacrifice I had put in made this moment so special. And this moment was not only for me, but for the entire country of Zambia, and everyone that has ever had a dream so big that it felt seemingly impossible, but they chose to go after it anyway. When I called Hannah to let her know, I knew her well enough to hold the phone away from my ear before she screamed her congratulations from the other end of the line. Then I made a few other calls—to my dad in Zambia and friends who knew I was taking the test that day. As Hannah and I sat together that night, eating a nice dinner at Capital Grille, it was surreal to look back at the number of times I almost gave up on this dream.

When I received an official letter from the Professional Golfers' Association of America congratulating me and recognizing me as the first Zambian to earn membership, I called my dad and read the entire letter to him. I thanked him for doing everything he had for me. This was the first time I said, "I love you, Dad," as I asked him to put my mom on the phone, so I could tell her the same. I promised to give her back the money she took out of her savings account. The excitement was not only from the accolade itself but also from the confirmation that I finished what I started.

Soon after that, I started receiving messages from all over the world. The news in Zambia showed a video of me opening my letter of recognition. My former schools in the UK sent me congratulatory messages as did a representative from the Royal & Ancient. But it was, unsurprisingly, an emotional note from Jonathan that meant the most to me.

Jonathan reflected on the first thoughts he had when he received my first letter from Zambia. He had felt my passion on paper then, and once he met me, he had seen it manifested and then grow tenfold. He was proud that my dream, which "so easily couldn't have been," had come to fruition.

Receiving PGA plaque

My story grew even bigger when PGA magazine released an article with the title "One in 17 Million, Zambia's Vincent Kabaso's Journey to PGA membership has been historic." This was followed by a shout out from a US congressman on television. Then I had a four-page spread feature in *Golf Digest* magazine with the headline: "Path of a Dreamer, How I Became the First PGA Professional from Zambia."

I realized, through the letters of recognition and media coverage, how much my story meant to others. A man named Jim, who read the *Golf Digest* article, wrote to me about his late father's own adventures living and working in the Zambian copper mines. Teachers and coaches invited me to speak to their students and athletes about resilience, pressing forward, and taking ownership of their journeys through life. In an interview on SiriusXM with David Marr, I discussed how, as a child, my social status made me feel second class and like I didn't have any business dreaming big dreams. But now that I had succeeded, I wanted any young men and women listening to me to see beyond their limits and understand the world is theirs for the taking.

My purpose, I realized, was bigger than I had originally thought. I had the ability to reach and inspire people beyond the world of golf. This was a very humbling moment for anybody who has ever conquered a mountain. Through Raised by the World Foundation, I promised myself to set a legacy of ubuntu, reaching out and helping to make the dreams of many dreamers come true.

Mom with Hannah's parents

I found a new home when I was hired as a PGA first assistant at Laurel Creek Country Club in New Jersey. And then our baby, JoAnna Zawadi Kabaso, was born on September 19 at 7:23 a.m. We had decided not to find out the gender, so it was a happy surprise when we saw it was a girl! We decided to name her JoAnna after our moms (Hannah's mom, Jo, and my mom, Anna), and Zawadi, a

Swahili name meaning *gift*. She indeed was a pleasant gift given to us at a moment of great excitement in our lives.

While Hannah was on maternity leave, we made arrangements for my mother to come to America, her first trip anywhere. It is a shared dream of many Africans who've made themselves a life in the Western world to give their parents the opportunity to travel and experience a new world and lifestyle. Facilitating a trip for my mother to come to the United States was truly an honor and a humbling experience for me.

I was anxiously waiting at John F. Kennedy airport's international arrivals section when I saw my mom in a fancy suit, walking alongside the other travelers. I hadn't seen her in almost five years. We embraced, and I complimented her for being able to navigate through customs. With some deep breaths, she told me she had been asked to go to a holding room for some questions about items she had in her bag before being allowed into the country.

The dry green vegetable called *chibwabwa* she brought with her apparently resembled cannabis, and the white ground soda powder commonly used to spice all kinds of foods looked like cocaine! My mother, who could barely understand what the uniformed men and women were asking, could only vaguely explain that those items were used for making the African delicacies *ifisashi* and *polony chikanda*. Though not funny at first, the further away from the airport we got, the more we found ourselves laughing about it.

The drive home took a little over an hour. It was very special for me to see the shock and awe reflected in my mother's eyes as she experienced the tall buildings, endless streetlights, and eight-lane highways for the first time. I was reminded not to take these blessings for granted, and I remembered how impressed I had been during my own travels over the years. This incredulous look continued until we arrived at my house where my mom saw JoAnna for the first time and was instantly in familiar territory once more. Hannah looked on nervously as my mother picked JoAnna up with one hand, and I calmly held up eight fingers to remind my wife how many kids my mother had raised.

Christmas time with the family

And at that moment, I felt calm. I couldn't remember the last time my body and mind were both fully relaxed like this. Most of my life, the fear of failure kept me on edge and was my biggest source of motivation. Many of my decisions were based on running from what I didn't want to become and searching for a way out. But as I looked over at my trusting wife, my knowing mother, and my baby daughter, content that I had achieved my dream, I knew that my experience was a story that had to be told. It had to be known that my success didn't just happen, that it was a result of hard work, to show that anything and everything is possible. We proved that there is always a way, and until this message reaches the most disadvantaged, it will remain my mission to share my journey.

INDEX

CPSIA information can be obtained
at www.ICGtesting.com
Printed in the USA
LVHW110745241120
672559LV00005B/313